Methods to Improve AI Code Generation

Mohd Rashid

Abstract

In recent years, transformer-based AI language models have gained prominence due to their powerful capabilities in a variety of tasks including generation of images, video, text and code. Large Language Models (LLMs) exist with parameters counts of a trillion parameters and greater. Such models are proprietary and unavailable for organizations to deploy privately. Even if such deployments were possible, the tremendous resource requirements of LLMs preclude their deployment on infrastructure smaller than enterprise and hyper-scale data centers. Small Language Models (SLMs), with far lower parameter counts of billions or fewer are a viable alternative for use on small servers and edge devices including PCs. While SLMs possess similar generative capabilities as LLMs, the reduction in model size is correlated with a decrease in accuracy when evaluated across a broad range of generative applications, including code generation in multiple languages.

To mitigate this shortcoming, an SLM may be fine-tuned with a curated code dataset consisting of code examples in a target programming language. This praxis presents results illustrating how two fine-tuned SLMs variants have been created that improve average accuracy in C++ code generation by more than 9%, and Rust code generation by more than 14%.

Fine-tuning a model to improve its accuracy on a task such as code generation in one language may reduce the output quality of the fine-tuned model in other areas, such as code generation in another language, or prose text generation. To overcome this tradeoff in generation quality, a novel SLM ensemble architecture was created for this praxis. This router-based ensemble encapsulates multiple fine-tuned specialist code models.

At inference time, a model is selected as the most likely to produce optimal output for a given prompt. This model is then used to generate the final result.

This praxis defines the problem space of code generation with SLMs and provides an in-depth review of the methods used to create the ensemble model, the experimental methodology, and the significant capability improvements shown in the results. A notable finding is that by employing an ensemble of fine-tuned coding SLMs, average code generation accuracy in C++ and Rust is improved by more than 10% compared to an off-the-shelf SLM.

Table of Contents

Chapter 1
Introduction

1.1 Background

Transformer-based language models can perform diverse tasks ranging from image generation and writing poetry to generating source code, but output quality depends on model size, which is a function of parameter count. Large Language Models (LLMs) such as OpenAI's code-davinci-002 (GPT-3 175B), can produce high-quality output in generative coding tasks including writing and summarizing computer programs - but the size of such models prevents their use on edge devices such as PCs and smartphones. To unlock the potential of generative AI on commodity hardware, Small Language Models (SLMs) were developed. These models contain just 2B to 14B parameters but are still capable of performing diverse tasks. "Phi-3 small (7bn) … achieves language understanding and commonsense reasoning on par with and code generation scores running up to 70bn models of the same generation." (Belcak et al., 2025, p3) "… humans balance computational efficiency with practical embodiment. SLMs, by analogy, are systems compact enough to run on personal devices" (Belcak et al., 2025, p15)

Language models manifest an engineering tradeoff between generative output accuracy and model size. For models of the same architecture but of different sizes – SLM and LLM versions of the same model – the SLM output quality is lower. Transformer-based models have developed rapidly during the past several years and excel at coding tasks including code completion, code generation, bug fixing and test generation (see Section 2.2.1 Code Generation Using Small Language Models.) Current-generation transformer models are capable of zero-shot, one-shot and few-shot learning.

Their generative capabilities show that an optimally trained model can generalize knowledge and produce new content without a necessity to fine-tune the model for every target application.

1.2 Problem Statement

"SLMs lack sufficient generality of knowledge to generate effective code for diverse real-world use cases, preventing software development productivity gains that could save significant costs." (Jovanović, 2024, p. 97) (Fakhoury, 2024, p. 2263)

Considering that transformer-based language models encode knowledge in the form of layers of artificial neurons and their associated weights and biases, recent LLM development efforts have resulted in larger models with an exponential size increase as measured by parameter count. For example, OpenAI's GPT 4.5 is estimated to contain about 1.5 trillion parameters. Such models are suitable for deployment only in hyper-scale data centers with large numbers of GPUs, TPUs or other powerful inference hardware. Due to their proprietary status, models in this class are not available for private deployment.

By contrast, SLMs are orders of magnitude smaller. Microsoft's *Phi-3 small* model contains just 7 billion parameters. Although SLMs take advantage of optimization techniques like *Flash Attention*, since the model's knowledge is stored in the form of parameters, a significantly lower parameter count means much less knowledge is stored in the model, and therefore there is less information the model can draw upon when performing inference. (Dao-AILab, n.d.)

Human intelligence may be augmented by use of an AI coding assistant to auto-complete functions, methods or complete code modules – saving time. Since developer time is costly, this translates directly into cost savings for software companies and other organizations that develop software. There are several factors that decrease a developer's capacity to take full advantage of LM generative coding capabilities.

First, use of an LLM requires API access to a cloud service that provides the code generation capability. This means that necessary context about the objective to be fulfilled by the code must be transmitted over the internet to an endpoint for processing. One example of such context is fragments of source code to be completed by the AI model. Since source code may include proprietary data or algorithms, the need to interact with an API can result in sensitive data, including protected intellectual property, being compromised by sharing it with a third party. Models hosted by commercial cloud providers such as AWS or OpenAI generate source code that organizations can incorporate into their products and other intellectual property.

When a developer uses an AI service to generate code via an Integrated Development Environment (IDE), the cloud API calls can be replaced with integration of a locally hosted SLM on the edge device (PC). For this solution to be effective, SLMs must meet the bar for effective generation capability in an appropriate programming language and problem domain. For example, for a developer building an image processing utility in Python, the SLM must be skilled in Python code generation, and be familiar with how to use common image processing libraries.

Second are resource issues, including cost. Due to the high compute requirements for AI inference, requiring GPUs or custom silicon like TPUs, such costs are relatively high (Google Cloud, n.d.). Since the goal is to reduce costs by utilizing AI to increase coding velocity, but the cost to do so is high, this can offset or even negate cost savings.

When considering SLMs as an alternative to costly cloud LLMs, evaluating the tradeoffs in generative capability is important. SLMs are proficient at executing complex coding tasks like code completion and prompt-based code generation, but due to the challenges outlined above, smaller models may not be sufficient to meet the challenges of many real-world problems. This praxis develops a novel ensemble architecture, composed of multiple SLMs fine-tuned on specialized code datasets, that improves output quality while also addressing privacy and IP protection concerns.

1.3 Book Statement

"An ensemble of SLMs fine-tuned on customized code datasets will improve average C++ and Rust code generation accuracy by at least 10% compared to an off-the-shelf SLM- increasing software development productivity."

When a single language model is used to perform code completion through IDE integration, the IDE will continuously prompt the model during development to generate code. The output quality of the model is limited by the size and architecture of the model, as well as the data that has been used to train the model. The results presented in Chapter 4 demonstrate that significant improvements in code generation performance can be achieved by combining multiple fine-tuned language models in an ensemble. The ensemble architecture is such that, at generation time, the model that is expected to produce the best output will be selected to perform the actual code generation.

Several products from this praxis are provided in Appendix B: Models, Code and Data Sets, including the source code for the ensemble model and model artifacts for each of the fine-tuned models. Source code for fine-tuning is also made available.

AI developers will be able to integrate the resulting ensemble code generation model into software running on edge devices. As the SLMs that make up the ensemble are relatively small (on the order of 7 billion parameters), they will be suitable for performing code generation tasks on PCs with consumer-grade GPUs.

1.4 Research Questions

This section introduces the research questions that frame the goals of this praxis. The questions are derived from the objective stated in the book statement: to show that an *ensemble of SLMs fine-tuned on customized code datasets will improve average C++ and Rust code generation accuracy by at least 10% compared to an off-the-shelf SLM - increasing software development productivity*. The three questions focus sequentially on several key aspects, where positive results for the first two questions lead into the third question. Results supporting the third question will also support the book statement. As discussed in detail in Chapter 3, the HumanEvalPack benchmark provides a standard framework to measure code generation performance in multiple languages – including the two languages chosen for this praxis, C++ and Rust.

RQ1 Will a fine-tuned SLM demonstrate statistically significant improvement in the HumanEvalPack benchmark score for coding in C++, compared to an off-the-shelf SLM?

RQ2 Will a fine-tuned SLM demonstrate statistically significant improvement in the HumanEvalPack benchmark score for coding in Rust, compared to an off-the-shelf SLM?

RQ3 Will a fine-tuned SLM ensemble demonstrate statistically significant improvement in the HumanEvalPack benchmark score for coding in both

C++ and Rust, compared to an off-the-shelf SLM?

The first research question focuses on comparing the performance in C++ code generation for an off-the-shelf SLM to a fine-tuned variant of this SLM. The second research question addresses the related problem of comparing the performance of Rust code with a fine-tuned SLM - versus an off-the-shelf SLM. The HumanEvalPack coding benchmark will be used to evaluate the model performance.

For the third question the research centers on a comparison of code generation performance in multiple languages of an ensemble of fine-tuned SLMs, compared to a single off-the-shelf SLM. An ensemble is a group of SLMs preceded in the system architecture by a router, which decides based on an evaluation of the prompt which model is expected to produce the best result for a given input prompt. The preferred model then generates code from the prompt.

1.5 Research Hypotheses

This section introduces the research hypotheses that proceed from the research questions and establish concrete thresholds that must be met to support each hypobook. Each hypobook corresponds to one research question, addressing a specific aspect of code generation with SLMs. The three hypotheses sequentially address the problem space of fine-tuning models to improve code generation in individual languages and culminate by addressing improved generative coding in multiple languages, using an ensemble of SLMs.

H1 The HumanEvalPack pass@10 benchmark score will increase by a percentage of at least 7% using a fine-tuned SLM for C++ code generation, versus an off-the-shelf SLM.

H2 The HumanEvalPack pass@10 benchmark score will increase by a percentage of at least 7% using a fine-tuned SLM for Rust code generation, versus an off-the-shelf SLM.

H3 The average HumanEvalPack pass@10 benchmark score will increase by a percentage of at least 10% using an ensemble of fine-tuned SLMs for C++ and Rust code generation, versus an off-the-shelf SLM.

Research hypotheses 1 and 2 state that the benchmark score for the HumanEvalPack benchmark score will increase when using a fine-tuned SLM, versus an off-the-shelf SLM. An independent variable for this hypobook is the choice of the model, such as Phi-3-Small or Mistral 7B. The architecture and stored knowledge in the model are key drivers for the ultimate code generation result. Another input variable is the choice of the training dataset for the fine-tuning. The prompt style (see Section 3.3.1 Prompting Approaches) is another input variable. The dependent variable is the set of results from HumanEvalPack benchmark execution.

For research hypobook 3, an independent variable is the set of fine-tuned models used in the ensemble. The dependent variable is the average pass@10 measurement for multiple languages C++ and Rust.

1.6 Organization of Praxis

The structure of this praxis provides a framework to define the research focus and goals, contextualize the research with related work, and present the scientific experiments and techniques employed during execution and analysis. The praxis progresses from a definition of the research area, establishes context through a review of prior work, and comprehensively describes the methodology, results and conclusions. Chapter 1 introduces the problem space of code generation using language models and defines the book, research questions and research hypotheses. Chapter 2 surveys the landscape of scholarship in the area of study. Chapter 3 details the methodology used during execution, including the techniques used to fine-tune language models, create an ensemble model, collect results and analyze those results. Chapter 4 presents the results of the praxis and analyzes the significance of these results. In Chapter 5 the conclusions from the research are presented, including a summary of how the conclusions support the book. Future work stemming from the praxis is also outlined in this chapter.

Chapter 2
Book Review

2.1 Introduction

This chapter presents a review of the scholarly corpus relevant to the topic of enhancing small language model code generation capabilities using fine-tuned model ensembles. The starting point is a definition of the fundamental attributes of Small Language Models (SLMs). Following that is an overview of code language models and AI coding tasks. The subsequent section surveys state-of-the-art techniques for evaluation of code generated by language models – with additional details on the approaches applied in this research. The next section consists of a review of existing work framing the problem space of language model ensembles. The final section explores modern approaches to enhance code generation by fine-tuning language models.

2.2 Small Language Models

Popular Large Language Models (LLMs) such as GPT-5, Gemini and Claude are proprietary models that are available for public use in generative inference tasks. These LLMs are hosted in centralized hyper-scale data centers and are not made available for private deployment. Containing up to trillions of parameters, their use in resource-constrained environments is not feasible.

The growth of LLMs over time follows a scalability pattern of increasing parameter count and number of layers that runs counter to resource efficiency. The size of LLMs effectively prevents their deployment on resource-constrained devices. Other challenges to pervasive deployment of LLMs include the financial cost of training such large models, hallucinations, and bias replication. (Zhang, Liu, & Pan, 2025) (Jovanovic & Campbell, 2024)

$$P_\theta(\mathbf{y} \mid \mathbf{x}) \Rightarrow P_\theta(\mathbf{y} \mid \text{prompt}(\mathbf{x}, \{(\mathbf{x}_i, \mathbf{y}_i)\}_{i=1}^{k})), k \in \{0, 1, \ldots, M\}$$

(A) Formulation of code generation by a language model. Reprinted from (Jiang, Wang, Shen, Kim, & Kim, 2024, p1:8)

$$\textbf{Greedy Search}: \mathbf{y}^* = \underset{\mathbf{y}}{\operatorname{argmax}} P_\theta(\mathbf{y} \mid \text{prompt}(\mathbf{x}, \{(\mathbf{x}_i, \mathbf{y}_i)\}_{i=1}^{k})), k \in \{0, 1, \ldots, M\}$$

(B) Greedy search to derive output from code generation outputs. Reprinted from (Jiang, Wang, Shen, Kim, & Kim, 2024, p1:8)

$$\textbf{Sampling}: \mathbf{y} \sim P_\theta(\mathbf{y} \mid \text{prompt}(\mathbf{x}, \{(\mathbf{x}_i, \mathbf{y}_i)\}_{i=1}^{k})), k \in \{0, 1, \ldots, M\}$$

(C) Sampling from output distribution for code generation. Reprinted from (Jiang, Wang, Shen, Kim, & Kim, 2024, p1:8)

$$\mathbf{y} \sim P_\theta(\mathbf{y} \mid \text{prompt}(\mathbf{x}, \{(\mathbf{x}_i, \mathbf{y}_i)\}_{i=1}^{k}, \mathbf{y}_{pre}, \textbf{Feedback}(\textbf{Exe}(\mathbf{y}, \mathcal{T})))), k \in \{0, 1, \ldots, M\}$$

(D) Formulation of LLM code generation, incorporating execution and test feedback. Reprinted from (Jiang, Wang, Shen, Kim, & Kim, 2024, p1:9)

$$\text{pass@}k := \underset{\text{Problems}}{\mathbb{E}} \left[1 - \frac{\binom{n-c}{k}}{\binom{n}{k}} \right]$$

(E) pass@k metrics. Reprinted from (Kulal et al., 2019)

Figure 1: Formulas (A – E)

Small Language Models (SLMs) are a viable alternative. They are appropriately sized for resource-constrained edge devices such as PCs. As shown in the results of this praxis (see Chapter 4—Results and Discussion), the efficiency and tractability advantage of applying SLMs can be amplified in two ways. First, models can be fine-tuned for specific code-generation applications. Second, multiple fine-tuned SLM models can be combined into a router-based ensemble. "SLMs aim to be more compact, efficient, specialized, and accessible while still retaining useful language understanding and generation capabilities." (Jovanovic & Campbell, 2024, p96) "SLMs typically range from 1 million to 10 billion parameters. Despite being significantly smaller, SLMs have shown effective performance on domain-specific tasks such as code generation." (Hasan et al., 2025, p1)

SLMs have advantages in terms of efficiency, accessibility, customization, safety and privacy. Each of these advantages apply to the use of SLMs in this praxis. First, efficiency improvements remove barriers to usage of SLMs on lower-powered, commodity hardware like desktop PCs. "... it is impractical to deploy a model with 70B parameters on a personal office laptop." (Xu et al., 2024, p8) Second, SLMs can be fine-tuned at a lower cost than LLMs. As shown in this praxis, a single Nvidia 5090 GPU, with an MSRP of $1999 and 32GB of VRAM, is sufficient to fine-tune the Phi-3-small SLM, which has 7 billion parameters. (NVIDIA, 2025). In contrast, fine-tuning even a relatively small LLM such as the Llama-3.1 variant with 70 billion parameters, requires more than 40GB of VRAM. (Meta, 2025) This requires a GPU with more memory, such as the Nvidia RTX Pro 6000 with 96 GB of VRAM – at a cost of $8565. (Hassam, 2025)

Security for proprietary data is improved, and privacy concerns are mitigated with SLMs, since they can be deployed on private infrastructure, including edge devices. SLMs also do not require sharing of proprietary, sensitive or controlled data with a commercial cloud service provider. (Zhang, Liu, & Pan, 2025)

The process of creating an SLM consists of four stages. First, during the input processing stage, the model developer prepares and extracts labelled or unlabeled training data, including modalities such as natural language text, images, or program code. The next stage, model development, entails fine-tuning, instruction tuning, or Reinforcement Learning from Human Feedback (RLHF). Next, output processing enables model output refinement using performance benchmarks. Once a model has been created, it is hosted for use in an inference server or locally on an edge device. (Jovanovic & Campbell, 2024).

In this praxis, the *HumanEvalPack-Synthesize* benchmark suite is employed for performance evaluation. This benchmark is designed to evaluate code generation in multiple languages, including C++ and Rust, by employing the same standard test methodology that was established in the *HumanEval* benchmark. *HumanEvalPack-Synthesize* extends this approach to support multiple languages, instead of only Python. *HumanEvalPack-Synthesize* consists of a set of human-written prompts for each supported programming language. For each coding prompt the benchmark includes a corresponding unit test that validates the correctness of the generated solution. The result of the benchmark execution is the standard pass@k metric, which measures code generation performance. Further detail about this benchmark is provided below in Section 2.3 Evaluation of Code Generation Language Models.

Another key concern is the hardware infrastructure and software architecture needed for edge generative AI applications using SLMs. Smaller edge models can collaborate with larger, centralized models to optimize efficiency, latency and output quality for various applications. A key application of SLMs is specialized fine-tuning, which can be applied to scenarios including generative coding in a single programming language. One challenge to edge deployment of SLMs is a lack of mature best practices for fine-tuning.

Another issue is that the smaller context size (prompt length) of SLMs limits input expressivity. (Jovanovic & Campbell, 2024)

2.2.1 Code Generation Using Small Language Models

Language Models (LMs) support two broad categories of coding tasks: *Code Understanding* and *Code Generation.* Understanding tasks include code classification, bug detection and clone detection. In code classification, the LM analyzes a code snippet and assigns a label. Such labels identify the problem domain or application addressed by the code. In bug detection, the LM's task is to find functional defects in the logic or syntax of the code. In clone detection, the LM code is analyzed to find functional duplication, which could be replaced with better abstraction or code reuse. These three tasks are examples of code-to-label workflows, where the LM is prompted with a code sample, and the output is one or more labels.

Generation tasks include code completion, code translation and test generation. In code completion, the LM is prompted with a code sample, and will add content to finish the code, based on the LM's understanding of the code's purpose. This task corresponds to the *continue* prompt format used to benchmark models in this praxis (see Section 3.3.1 Prompting Approaches.) In code translation, the model is prompted with one code snippet, and outputs functionally equivalent code in another programming language. In code repair, the code snippet in the prompt is corrected to address defects as they are understood by the LM.

These three types of generation tasks are code-to-code tasks – because both the input and the output are source code. Code generation is a natural language to source code task. In this task, the prompt describes a coding problem, often including input and output examples, and the LM generates code to solve the problem. This task corresponds to the *instruct* prompt format used in this praxis. (Jiang, Wang, Shen, Kim, & Kim, 2024)

Both general-purpose LLMs like GPT-3 and coding-specific SLMs like Qwen2.5-Coder demonstrate strong code generation capabilities. (Brown et al., 2020) (Hui et al., 2024) General-purpose models may be pre-trained on large datasets, such as textbooks, book and other publications. Such pre-training datasets may also include a proportion of code data, and related material such as mathematical data. Coding-focused models may reverse this content proportion in the pre-training dataset, with more code and logic data, and less general-purpose text data. Coding-focused variants of general-purpose models can be developed using fine-tuning.

As shown in Figure 1 (A), given a model with parameters θ, the generation algorithm can be expressed as the probability of *y* given *x*. Here, *x* represents the natural language code generation prompt, and *y* represents the output, consisting of generated code. In this formula *k* represents *exemplars* that are appended to the input prompt. Such exemplars include sample input or output for the prompt, and restrictions to the output format. *k* specifies the number of learning shots, where k = 0 indicates zero-shot learning.

Learning shots are a measurement of the number of input-output examples included in a prompt. In generative AI, a zero-shot prompt relies on the knowledge already stored in the model to generate a result. A zero-shot prompt could ask the model to implement an algorithm (such as merge sort) in a specific programming language (such as C++). In a one-shot prompt, a single example would be included in the prompt – such as C++ code that implements an actual sorting algorithm. In a multi-shot prompt, more than one code example would be included in the prompt.

The *prompt* function denotes the string representation of the few-shot natural-language input. Figure 1 (B and C) show two approaches to selecting the final generative output from the output probabilities generated by the model. In the greedy search approach, the *argmax* function is used to select the output with the highest probability. In the *sampling* approach, shown in Figure 1 (B), temperature or top-k methods are applied to sample from the output distribution.

As shown in Figure 1 (D), additional validation steps follow the generation step: compilation (interpretation), execution of the generated code, and validation of the correctness of the solution via execution of unit tests. This approach is used in this research, with the HumanEvalPack test harness (see Section 2.3 Evaluation of Code Generation Language Models). *Exe* represents compilation or interpretation of the generated code in the target language, such as C++, Rust or Python. *Feedback* involves execution of unit tests on the generated code sample. The test outputs a binary result (pass / fail), showing whether the generated code has correctly solved the problem. The accuracy of the feedback is a factor of the robustness and correctness of each unit test.

2.3 Evaluation of Code Generation Language Models

HumanEval provides a complete framework for evaluation of code generated by language models. (Chen et al., 2021) This paper also describes a GPT (Generative Pretrained Transformer) model called Codex, which is trained specifically for code generation. While other models have surpassed the performance of Codex since 2021, when the paper was written, the HumanEval framework remains as a leading benchmark suite and evaluation methodology for measuring code generation performance. The focus is Python code generation, often using prompts written in the form of Python docstrings.

Considering that this praxis is focused on code generation in the Rust and C++ languages, applying the approach defined here along with the multi-language approach utilized in the *OctoPack* paper is appropriate. The HumanEval approach to evaluation of generated code uses prompts written by humans. "These problems assess language comprehension, algorithms, and simple mathematics, with some comparable to simple software interview questions." (Chen et al., 2021) The prompts are paired with unit tests also authored by humans that validate the correctness of the generated solution.

This approach supports a simple pass / fail metric for code generation, based on the prompt as input, and validation of the generated code based on the result of the unit test execution. The unit-test evaluation approach is contrasted in the paper with other, more general approaches such as exact or fuzzy matches, or BLEU score. "… match-based metrics are unable to account for the large and complex space of programs functionally equivalent to a reference solution." (Chen et al., 2021) In essence, there are many textual variations in program source code that can result in a correct, successful unit test execution result – and comparing various program text in a naive match-based fashion will not provide an appropriate comparison metric.

The HumanEval dataset consists of 164 human-written Python programming problems. A summary of the results of the full suite of tests in HumanEval is computed using the *pass@k* metric. For *k* program generations per prompt, an unbiased estimator provides a numerically stable summary value measuring generation accuracy. (Kulal et al., 2019)

The authors also explored the problem of docstring generation from code. A docstring is an inline annotation in source code that provides contextual documentation about what a method or function does, and what the expected input and output of the function are. Correct generation of a docstring for a code sample demonstrates that the LM understands the code and can enhance it by adding inline documentation. "Nevertheless, we are motivated to produce a docstring writing model for safety reasons, as such a model can be used to describe the intent behind generated code." (Chen et al., 2021)

The paper addresses potential economic impacts of code generation – which applies to this praxis's goal of achieving cost savings by improving code generation performance. While productivity can be improved by using generative AI tools, such usage can result in a reduction in collaboration among developers as they engage in group problem-solving.

Extending the approach established in HumanEval, the *OctoPack* paper describes the development of *HumanEvalPack*, a multi-language benchmark for evaluation of code generation. The paper describes the assembly and curation of a large code dataset (4 terabytes), including a vast array of code samples in 350 programming languages. Highly relevant to this praxis, the authors adopt and extend the structure of the original HumanEval benchmark – which consists of 164 programming problems in Python only. They engaged human coders to formulate 6 analogous sets of 164 problems – written in Python, JavaScript, Java, Go, C++ and Rust. This set of programming problems and unit tests, called *HumanEvalPack*, is the basis of the evaluation framework we employ in our work, along with *bigcode-evaluation-harness*, which is the test harness developed for OctoPack. (bigcode-project, n.d.) (Muennighoff et al., 2023).

The *OctoPack* work is also focused on instruction tuning. In instruction-tuned models, metadata fields in the ChatML format are included as structural elements in each training sample. This structure provides context to the model regarding the role of each sample – such as whether it is a prompt or a response. The code instruction dataset assembled and curated for *OctoPack* is called *CommitPack.* The authors note the usefulness of a pretraining approach using a data set that contains code in multiple languages, followed by instruction-formatted fine-tuning rounds that only include a subset of the languages used for pre-training. Even though the fine-tuning rounds contain only a subset of the languages, such fine-tuning improves coding performance overall. (Muennighoff et al., 2023)

The CommitPack dataset was retrieved from Google BigQuery, including both the code samples and metadata about the *git* commits used to develop the code. Based on the assumption that the size of instruct-formatted fine-tuning data can be much smaller than the raw pretraining data, they capture a 2 gigabyte subset of the 4 terabyte source GitHub data from BigQuery. The instruction format consists of a natural language instruction, followed by the code generation result. As shown in Section 3.4.2 Agentic Fine-Tuning, the same instruction format is used in this praxis when fine-tuning the Phi-3 model.

The evaluation framework selected for this research is the *HumanEvalSynthesize* benchmark from the *HumanEvalPack* project. The benchmarks are formulated as NL->C: natural language to code – corresponding to the original approach in *HumanEval.* The natural language prompt consists either of a docstring-type description of the task, or a task description embedded in comment syntax in the target language. As in Chen et al. (2021), the *pass@k* metric is employed to measure performance. This paper also covers two other approaches: *HumanEvalFix* and *HumanEvalExplain.* In the former, described as NL+C->C, the prompt consists of natural language instructions and code, and the generated output is *fixed* code: “Given an incorrect code function with a subtle bug and accompanying unit tests, the model is tasked to fix the function.” (Muennighoff et al., 2023).

The third code benchmark variant, *HumanEvalExplain*, is also formulated as NL+C->NL. Here the task is to summarize a code sample in natural language. Subsequently, a follow-on task will prompt the model to regenerate the original code, based on its own summary. This approach establishes a feedback loop to measure both code summarization, and code generation based on a summary. *HumanEvalSynthesize* is used in this research due to its simple structure and lower generation latency.

2.4 Ensembles of Language Models

The router-based SLM language model ensemble approach developed for this praxis enables software engineers to use SLMs to generate code on edge devices, improving developer productivity. As covered in Section 3.2 Models and Languages, two specialized fine-tuned models are employed, combined as an ensemble. Several related approaches to building language model ensembles for NLP are defined in Zhang & Shafiq (2024), p33, and the similarities between natural language text generation and code generation underscore the relevance of this book.

Three model ensemble approaches, which are frequently applied in classical machine learning models including decision trees and random forests, are *bagging*, *boosting* and *stacking*. In contrast, for this work in deep learning a router-based approach is used because it is a better match for the generative output required for code generation. Zhang & Shafiq (2024) address an NLP classification task, which is suitable for the traditional approach of bagging (bootstrap aggregation). In bagging, subsets of the training data are randomly selected, by sampling with replacement, and each subset is allocated to one of several models in the ensemble. The bagging approach is appropriate for cases where multiple weak learners are combined, with the goal of reducing variance. With bagging, the ensemble learners may be trained in parallel.

An expansion of the concept used in bagging is weight merging – which, unlike bagging, can also be used in generative AI. With weight merging, the model weights from two or more models are combined, often by averaging them. (Ashiga et al., 2025, p1)

A survey of ensemble learning techniques that "focuses on text and code generation tasks, which encompass diverse research areas like mathematical reasoning, question answering (QA), massive multitask language understanding (MMLU), and code generation" provides a detailed overview of the generative ensemble problem space. (Ashiga et al., 2025, p1) LMs can reflect biases in their training data – as well as reflecting variance in their generative results in terms of the level of knowledge expertise across subject areas. An LM may demonstrate superior coding ability in one programming language versus another.

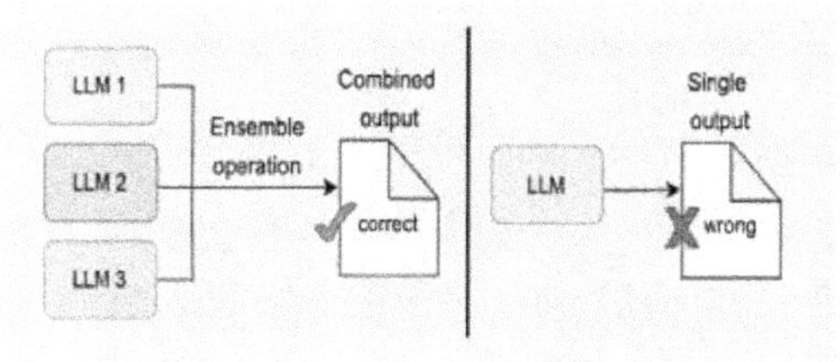

Figure 2: The difference between an ensemble LLM and a single LLM. Reprinted from (Ashiga et al., 2025, p2)

The two high-level categories of ensemble approaches are *Architectural-Level* and *Model-Level.* In the former, a single model is constructed from two or more constituent models. Architectural-level approaches include *Weight Merging* (as described above), *Knowledge Fusion, Mixture of Experts,* and the *Reward Ensemble.* In the latter, multiple full models are used in tandem. Model-level ensemble techniques include *Output Ensemble, Routing,* and *Cascading.*

In knowledge fusion, multiple source LLMs are processed to generate a probability matrix from the cross-entropy values in the output distribution of each LLM. Next, a fusing function is applied to each matrix, resulting in a single fused matrix. The fusing function will perform operations such as choosing the minimum or weighted average for each cross-entropy matrix element. The target LLM is then retrained using an objective function that integrates the fused matrix with weight of the target LLM – thereby enriching its knowledge with that of the source LLMs. To overcome differences in the respective tokenizers of the source and target models, dynamic programming approaches are employed to minimize the cost of transformer tokens from one tokenizer format to another. (Ashiga et al., 2025)

The *Mixture of Experts (MoE)* approach embeds multiple experts inside the model architecture. The MoE layer is preceded by a router layer – whose weights act as a gating function to apply appropriate experts, on a per-token basis. This approach increases parameter count and computational costs, but at a constant rate. MoE can mitigate issues such as a lack of expressive diversity in outputs, and inherent biases – which are linked to biases in training data used to create the model. *Switch Routing*, a related approach, directs a token to a single expert, which is cheaper in terms of computational cost. (Ashiga et al., 2025)

Another architectural approach, the *Reward Ensemble*, combines Reinforcement

Learning with Human Feedback (RLHF) with LLMs. In this ensemble type, a policy model is used with multiple reward models (RMs), an initial policy and a human preference dataset. During supervised fine-tuning or pretraining, the RMs are optimized and refined. Due to the multiple models involved, this type of ensemble can be computationally expensive, and so encoders may be shared to save resources among the parallel model executions. "This approach was introduced to address reward hacking (overoptimization), where a policy achieves high rewards while disregarding true human preferences" (Ashiga et al., 2025, p5)

In an *Output Ensemble*, a model-level ensemble, the same prompt is concurrently submitted to multiple LLMs. This results in multiple output instances, which are then combined or down selected to produce the final output. For classification problems, a voting algorithm such as *argmax* is applied to select a single preferred classification result. For generative approaches, including text generation, one more LLM is employed in the last pipeline phase to synthesize the outputs from each of the ensemble members. Alternatively, in a scoring model approach (another form of output ensemble), a classifier such as a Random Forest model can be trained to produce a confidence score from the LLM responses. Based on this score, the highest-ranking *k* results are returned. (Ashiga et al., 2025)

Routing Ensembles have one aspect in common with *Output Ensembles* – in both cases there are multiple LLMs in the ensemble that may be used to process each input prompt. With the routing approach, just one LLM from the ensemble is used – unlike the output ensemble approach, when multiple LLMs generate a response. The routing approach has a clear advantage in this regard, as executing a single generation is computationally cheaper. To choose which LLM will be used for generation, each prompt is assigned a score. The best choice for a scoring system depends on the problem domain and type – such as classification vs generation. For tasks like text summarization, a BART score can be used to produce the score. (Yuan, Neubig, & Liu, 2021) "This score is effective because it correlates well with the actual answers." (Ashiga et al., 2025, p6). Other transformer models, like RoBERTa can be used to produce a confidence score, which will be used for routing to a single LLM from the ensemble. For a confidence score to be sufficiently accurate, the scoring model needs to contain sufficient knowledge about the capabilities of the ensemble members.

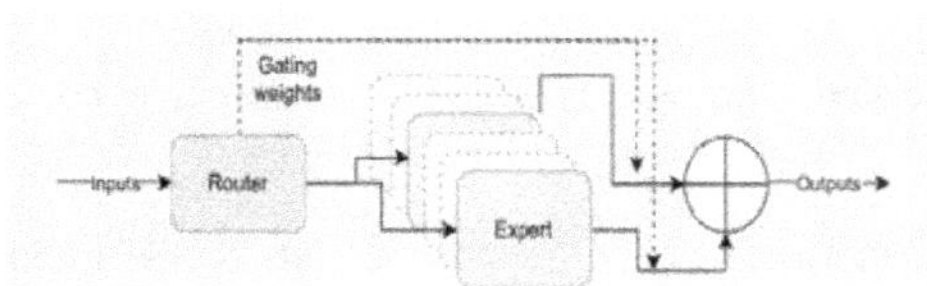

Figure 3: Router ensemble architecture. Reprinted from (Ashiga et al., 2025, p5)

A significant drawback of routers is reliance on the input data to select the most appropriate model to produce the final output from the ensemble – such as the classification or generation result. Since the input necessarily lacks the full context present in the output, there may not be sufficient information in the prompt a priori to make a sufficiently accurate model choice. This praxis shows how a novel variant of the routing approach can produce high-quality results for multiple language code-generation problems. By utilizing keyword matching based on sets of keywords found in the context-free grammar of C++ and Rust, an accurate choice can be made between a small number of ensemble members. This is a simpler yet more effective approach that is appropriate for the target uses cases in code generation, versus a cloud-scale router ensemble that encompasses several LLMs. As shown in Section 3.5 Ensemble

Architecture, fine-tuning an SLM to improve the quality of its expertise in multiple languages, which are then combined into a router-based ensemble, is an improved architecture for code generation in multiple languages.

2.5 Fine-Tuning

Bidirectional Encoder Representations from Transformers (BERT) is an influential transformer model that features innovations in the bidirectional self-attention mechanism. (Devlin, Chang, Lee, & Toutanova, 2019) BERT is designed to make the fine-tuning process straightforward, by applying the same process used in pre-training. As shown in Figure 4 below, as pairs of raw text sentences are used in the pre-training process, during fine-tuning pairs of related sentences can be used – such as a hypobook-premise pair.

Other transformer models, including decoder models like GPT and Phi-3 can be fine-tuned in a similar way. Due to the textual nature of program source code, this pair-wise approach for fine-tuning is applicable to SLMs like Phi-3 for code generation tasks. (Abdin et al., 2024)

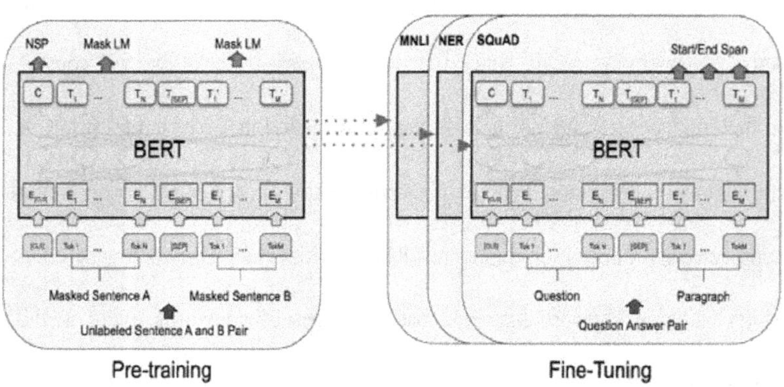

Figure 4: Pre-training and Fine-Tuning BERT. Reprinted from (Devlin, Chang, Lee, & Toutanova, 2019, p4173)

HumanEval and related benchmarks are essential for evaluation of code generation performance, especially in the context of fine-tuning language models. (Chen et al., 2021) OpenAI trained the 12B parameter GPT model using 179 GB of python files sourced from GitHub to produce the fine-tuned Codex python model. The Codex-12B model, containing 12 billion parameters, is of a similar order of magnitude in terms of model size as the Phi-3-small model that is fine-tuned in this research, at 7B parameters. Measuring performance of the Codex model using the *pass@100* metric, the authors show a 44.6% positive delta, compared to the GPT-J 6B result.

The authors also performed additional rounds of supervised fine-tuning for Codex after the GitHub python code fine-tuning. The dataset for this fine-tuning included problems and solutions from code contest websites and was followed by further fine- tuning with Continuous Integration (CI) data.

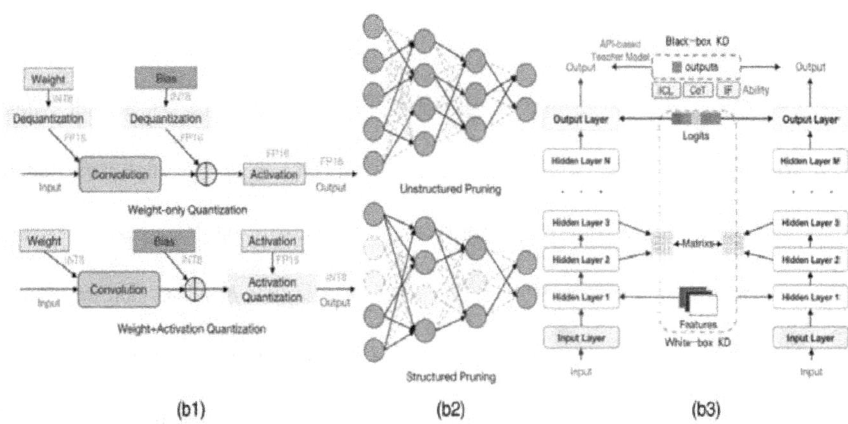

Figure 5: Model Compression approaches include Quantization (b1), Pruning (b2) and Distillation (b3). Reprinted from (Zhang, Liu, & Pan, 2025, p32)

The simplified model architectures of SLMs enable the training and fine-tuning process to be performed while requiring fewer computational resources than LLMs. (Zhang, Liu, & Pan, 2025) The authors also highlight compression techniques including quantization, pruning and model distillation. This paper also describes usage of *Efficient FFN* to mitigate quadratic scaling of memory utilization in the attention mechanism of transformer-based model architectures.

A Mixture of Experts (MoE) framework is incorporated to apply sub-parts of the model to process the input sequence. Another model optimization described in this paper is *Efficient Attention.* This approach includes applying sparse attention to "optimize computational efficiency by converting dense 2-D attention matrices into more manageable 1-D structures or by filtering out near-zero attention scores, thereby allowing the model to concentrate computational resources on pivotal interactions." (Zhang, Liu, & Pan, 2025, p33).

Quantization is another model compression technique that can provide gains in computational efficiency. When utilizing a GPU or other inference hardware that supports lower precision, higher bitrate weights (such as 16-bit floating point) are cast or truncated to lower bitrate weights (such as 8-bit integers). This can increase inference speed, albeit with commensurate trade-offs in accuracy. Next, *Pruning* is introduced as a method to decrease the size of model by deleting parts of the model that may be redundant. Finally, *Knowledge Distillation* utilizes a *teacher* and *student* designation for models, where knowledge encoded in the former model is extracted and integrated into the latter.

In *Black-box distillation* a teacher model is prompted to generate output, and the generated output is used to train the student model. As described in Chapter 3—Methodology, in this praxis agentic fine-tuning is employed to improve code generation in an SLM (Phi-3) by training it with code generations from a larger and much more powerful LLM (Gemini). *White-box* distillation is an alternative method, that is not directly applicable to this praxis, because it requires access to the intermediate representation internal to an LLM during the generation process.

"In addition to using SLMs alone, the collaboration of SLMs and LLMs can achieve better LLM training, fine-tuning, and adaptation." (Zhang, Liu, & Pan, 2025, p35) LLMs are trained on very large datasets, on the order of terabytes and higher. To adapt this approach for SLMs, which are limited in computational resources, curation and filtering of training data is employed. This approach consists of fine-tuning SLMs on filtered domain data, such as coding examples in a single programming language. This technique can feed back into the SLM training process, by improving training efficiency through use of smaller, more targeted training datasets. A related approach can be applied to adjust the output of a large model in its decoding layer. A small expert model can be used at this stage to tune the large model's output, using the specific domain knowledge encoding during the fine-tuning process of the smaller model.

2.6 Conclusion

As shown in this chapter, "SLMs aim to be more compact, efficient, specialized, and accessible while still retaining useful language understanding and generation capabilities." (Jovanovic & Campbell, 2024, p96). Despite a bias in germane scholarly book for coverage of the applications of LLMs, and LLM ensembles, the strong capabilities of SLMs for code generation support the conclusion that SLMs may benefit from ensemble architectures including routing ensembles. (Jiang, Wang, Shen, Kim, & Kim, 2024)

This book review has shown that the theoretical fundamentals of code generation when using LMs, as codified in Jiang, Wang, Shen, Kim, & Kim (2024), are valid for SLM ensembles. This conclusion is bolstered by the coding benchmark results in multiple languages in Muennighoff et al. (2023), using the *HumanEvalPack* benchmark suite – which is derived from the fundamental work by OpenAI et al in Chen et al. (2021), including the original *HumanEval* benchmark and the *pass@k* evaluation methodology.

Mixture of Experts (MoE) architectural ensemble and router ensemble approaches can upgrade model effectiveness through aggregation. (Ashiga et al., 2025) Finally, it has been shown that just as seminal models like BERT can be fine-tuned to significantly improve output quality for a specific domain, so can SLMs like Phi-3 be fine-tuned for tightly specified domains like code generation. This effectiveness of such fine-tuning is shown in the results presented in Chapter 4. (Zhang, Liu, & Pan, 2025)

Chapter 3
Methodology

3.1 Introduction

This chapter describes the methodology used in this praxis to improve AI generative coding performance in multiple languages, through fine-tuning. Several fine-tuned variants of off-the-shelf SLMs were created and assembled into an ensemble. As demonstrated through standard evaluation metrics, the single-language fine-tuned models each improve code generation by more than 7% in a single language - C++ and Rust, respectively. When these fine-tuned models are combined in an ensemble, they improve generation in both languages by an average of more than 10%. This supports the book statement: that an ensemble of fine-tuned SLMs will improve software development productivity.

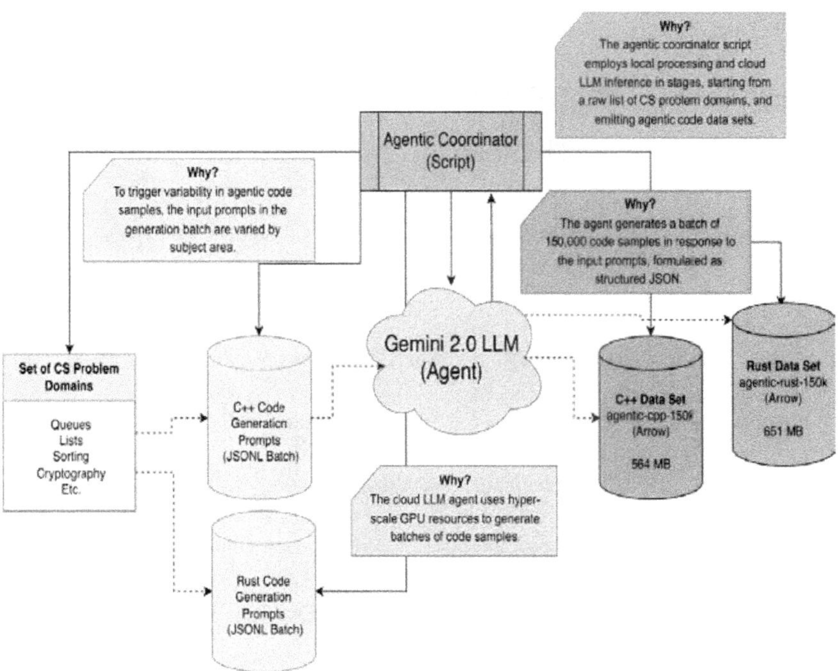

Figure 6: Methodology Map (Data)

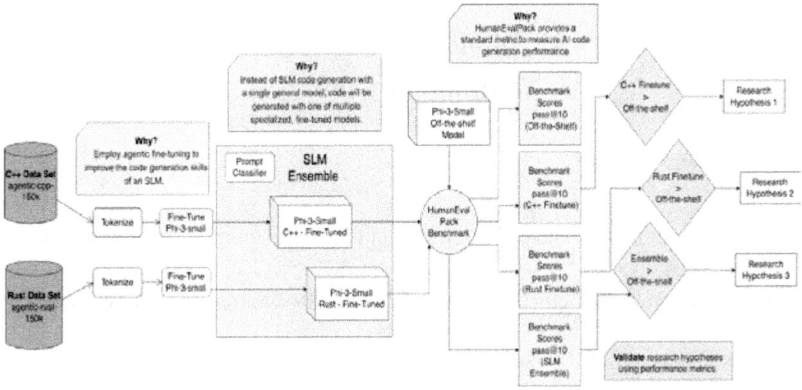

Figure 7: Methodology Map (Fine-Tuning and Evaluation)

Figure 6 and Figure 7 above provide an overview of the complete methodology for this praxis. Figure 6 shows how a set of computer science problem domains is used to construct a set of prompts for generation of training samples in two languages, C++ and Rust. An agentic coordination script employs the generative capacity of the Gemini 2.0 LLM to batch-process this set of prompts. The result is two datasets, one for C++ and another for Rust, that are structured for fine-tuning. This full process is detailed in Section 3.4 Data Sources and Fine Tuning.

The second part of the methodology map in Figure 7 shows how the two datasets are employed to fine-tune the Phi-3-small-128k SLM. This results in a collection of three Phi-3-based models: an off-the-shelf model, a Rust coding specialist model, and a C++ coding specialist model. These models can each be used individually or in combination as a router-based SLM ensemble. In the ensemble, a keyword-based prompt classifier decides which model from the ensemble collection will be used at inference time.

The measurement and evaluation framework (HumanEvalPack-Synthesize) is applied to measure the improvements in coding capabilities for each of the individual models, and the ensemble model. An analysis of these improvements will support the three research hypotheses, as detailed in the next chapter (Section 4.4 Hypobook Validation.)

Section 3.2 Models and Languages contains a survey of the language models that were evaluated and ultimately selected for the fine-tuning and ensemble creation process. This section also provides an overview of the suitability of these models for AI code generation in C++ and Rust. Next, in Section 3.3 Measurement and Evaluation, an in-depth treatment of the framework for measurement and evaluation of code generation performance is presented.

In Section 4, the data sources used for fine tuning, and the full agentic fine-tuning process is described, including usage of using standard libraries and an approach that builds upon existing fine-tuning techniques for the Phi-3 SLM. Section 3.5 Ensemble Architecture covers design and implementation of the router-based SLM ensemble architecture that is the primary focus of this praxis.

3.2 Models and Languages

This praxis is primarily focused on enhancing code generation in C++ and Rust, but the techniques employed are not limited to these languages. The fine-tuning approach and ensemble architecture can be expanded to other programming languages in future work. Phi-3 has been chosen as an appropriate model for AI code generation. This model, created by Microsoft, is publicly available as an open-weights model in several sizes and variants. The smallest variant, Phi-3-mini, contains 3.8 billion parameters, and Phi-3-small has 7 billion parameters. Since a modern desktop PC equipped with a GPU has sufficient compute capacity to perform generation with Phi-3-small-128k, it was used for fine-tuning, experimentation and evaluation. The *small* model variant's higher parameter count supports greater generation performance compared with the *mini* variant.

Measuring Phi-3-small's code generation performance, Microsoft's published benchmark results for the HumanEval python coding benchmark show zero-shot performance of 61.0%. (Abdin et al., 2024, p6) Other options for open-weight SLMs of a similar size are available, such as Mistral 7b, which also contains 7 billion parameters. However, as shown in the same benchmark table Mistral 7b scores only 28.0% on the same HumanEval benchmark – a reduction of 33% compared to Phi-3-small. (Abdin et al., 2024, p6)

Supporting the decision to proceed with Phi-3, another SLM in the same class, Gemma 7b, from Google, scores only 34% on the HumanEval benchmark. Additionally, although the Phi-3-medium variant of the model exists, with a 14 billion parameter count, the size of this model makes it less suitable for use on edge devices like smartphones or laptops. *HumanEval* coding benchmark scores show a performance increase of only a few percentage points compared to Phi-3-small. As noted in Abdin et al. (2024), p3, this suggests that the training data used is not optimal for the 14 billion parameter model size. This qualifies the 7 billion parameter size as an optimal choice for this project.

As described in Section 3.3 Measurement and Evaluation, the *HumanEval* Python coding benchmarks suggest that that Phi-3-small may be a suitable candidate for generative AI coding tasks for other languages as well, due to similar language structures. Based on these strong performance numbers on HumanEval, Phi-3-small has been selected for fine-tuning SLMs and creating an ensemble model composed of multiple fine-tuned SLMs. Considering this focus on the Phi-3 model, it is appropriate to review its architecture and the procedures used to train it.

The data and training methodology used to create a language model is a significant driver in the model's real-world performance on a diverse range of tasks. (Abdin et al., 2024, p1) Broadly speaking, the scaling laws indicate that higher performance can be achieved by creating larger LLMs over time, exponentially scaling the parameter count of the model – while improving training data and methodology. Running counter to this approach, the capabilities of small language models can also be scaled by training them with focused, optimal data sets. As noted in Abdin et al. (2024), optimality in this context indicates that the training and fine-tuning data used is filtered with respect to appropriate knowledge – for example, web data on a relevant subject. Phi-3 has also been trained with LLM-filtered data - which drives its outstanding performance on benchmarks. As demonstrated in Section 3.4.1 , the results fine-tuning Phi-3 reinforce the usefulness of this *data optimal* training approach. Phi-3 is a 32-head, 32-layer decoder-only transformer model. Most of the network layers consist of a blocksparse self-attention module, followed by a multi-layer perceptron (MLP) module, and then apply layer normalization to the output.

3.3 Measurement and Evaluation

When measuring the accuracy and effectiveness of a model for AI code generation, it is necessary to consider where requirements differ from other AI tasks like generation of natural language text or images. The implementation of an algorithm in code is designed by a programmer to perform a specific computation. For example, in sorting algorithms, which are typically deterministic, for a given input consisting of an ordered set of numbers, a correct implementation such as merge sort will output a list of the input in sorted order. To evaluate the correctness of such an implementation generated by a language model, the generated code must be executed. The output of the code for a given input sample can then be examined to check correctness.

Some flaws in the generated code can be detected before execution. For example, syntax errors in the code will result in the compiler or interpreter failing to parse or compile the generated code. Other coding errors may be detected during compilation – such as use of a non-existent (or undeclared) library dependency, a non-existent standard library function, type errors, or calling a function or method with incorrect parameters.

Modern software engineering practices dictate the use of automated testing to validate code correctness. As software engineers develop code modules, they may concurrently develop unit tests to validate the correctness of the module. Unit tests can be executed at compile time with a build tool, to ensure that newly developed code functions correctly, and that regressions are not accidentally introduced later during the development process. The robustness and completeness of each unit test influences the completeness of the test-based validation approach.

When evaluating code generated by SLMs, a similar procedure can be applied. Human programmers create sets of prompts for code generation problems and write unit tests that will validate that generated code has successfully solved the problem. The *HumanEval* coding benchmark suite is often used to measure code generation performance, and performance on this benchmark is included in many language model benchmarks. "We evaluate functional correctness on a set of 164 hand-written programming problems, which we call the HumanEval dataset. Each problem includes a function signature, docstring, body, and several unit tests, with an average of 7.7 tests per problem." (Chen et al., 2021) See Section 2.3 Evaluation of Code Generation Language Models for additional details.

Since the goal of this research is to improve code generation in C++ and Rust, a benchmark framework that supports these languages is required. The *HumanEvalPack* framework is an appropriate choice, supporting code generation evaluation in five languages in addition to Python: C++, Rust, Java, JavaScript and Go. (Muennighoff et al., 2023) The *HumanEvalSynthesize* task follows the same pattern used in Python for HumanEval: a prompt is submitted to the model describing a coding task, and unit tests are executed against the generated code to validate its correctness. Two additional task types are supported along with HumanEvalSynthesize: *HumanEvalFix* and *HumanEvalExplain.* In the former, a coding sample containing an intentional bug is provided in the prompt. The model is then tasked to fix the bug, and unit tests validate the correctness of the fix. In the latter, the model is prompted to explain the operation of a code sample. That explanation is then used as a prompt to regenerate the original code, and the regenerated code is validated in the same manner described above, to determine correctness of the regenerated code. This approach indirectly measures the quality of the generated code explanation. Since the subject of this praxis is generation of code from prompts and code completion, only the HumanEvalSynthesize benchmark was used.

The HumanEvalPack benchmark is executed by the *bigcode-evaluation-harness* framework. This tool is a generic AI code generation test harness that supports a wide range of state-of-the-art AI coding benchmarks. "BigCode is a community project jointly led by Hugging Face and ServiceNow. Both organizations committed research, engineering, ethics, governance, and legal resources to ensure that the collaboration runs smoothly and makes progress towards the stated goals. ServiceNow Research and Hugging Face have made their respective compute clusters available for large-scale training of the BigCode models, and Hugging Face hosts the datasets, models, and related applications from the community to make it easy for everyone to access and use." (BigCode: The mission, 2025)

In addition to HumanEvalPack, *bigcode-evaluation-harness* supports other frameworks including MBPP, APPS and CoNaLa. This research effort exclusively uses HumanEvalPack-Synthesize. This benchmark is executed against the Phi-small-128k base model, the fine-tuned variants of Phi-3-small-128k created for the praxis, and the ensemble of fine-tuned models. *Bigcode-evaluation-harness* uses three standard Python machine learning libraries from HuggingFace: Transformers, Accelerate, and Datasets. The Transformers library provides a standard interface for loading a generative model along with its associated tokenizer. This library is also used to drive the model when performing inference. The Accelerate library is a parallelization layer for PyTorch and the Transformers library. It supports sharding models and executing them in parallel on multiple GPUs. The Datasets library implements the standard HuggingFace interface for loading datasets, which is used to load the set of HumanEvalPack prompts and unit tests. Bigcode-evaluation-harness also supports compilation of the generated output programs, and running the associated unit tests for each, using a standard C++ and Rust compiler.

As covered in Section 2.3 Evaluation of Code Generation Language Models, the results from bigcode-evaluation-harness and humaneval-pack-synthesize benchmarks are expressed in terms of the pass@k metric, which depends on three key variables. *k* is the minimum number of generations that are performed for each of the 164 unit tests in the HumanEvalPack-Synthesize suite. The task in this case is one of the unit tests. *n* is the total number of samples generated per task. *c* is the number of correct generations for each task. The pass@k metric is an unbiased estimator. The research experiments were performed using a standard value of $k = 10$. For each benchmark execution, at least 10 code samples are generated for each unit test.

3.3.1 Prompting Approaches

When executing code generation benchmarks with HumanEvalPack-Synthesize, there is a bifurcation of results correlated with the prompt style. *Bigcode-evaluation-harness* supports several prompt styles. In this research, only two are employed for benchmarks: *continue* and *instruct*. *Continue* is a code completion prompt. In this style, the model is prompted with a snippet of code, such as a method signature, and instructions for how to complete the code. The instructions are embedded in comments in the code snippet. Figure 8 shows an example of a continue prompt for Java. In this case, a class skeleton with standard imports is provided, named *Solution*, that contains a single method signature – *hasCloseElements*. The model is expected to follow the instructions in the comment block above the method signature and implement the method as indicated.

```
import java.util.*;
import java.lang.*;

class Solution {
    /**
    Check if in given list of numbers, are any two numbers closer to each other than given threshold.
    >>> hasCloseElements(Arrays.asList(1.0, 2.0, 3.0), 0.5)
    false
    >>> hasCloseElements(Arrays.asList(1.0, 2.8, 3.0, 4.0, 5.0, 2.0), 0.3)
    true
     */
    public boolean hasCloseElements(List<Double> numbers, double threshold ) {

```

Figure 8: Continue prompt example

```
Write a Java function `public boolean hasCloseElements(List<Double> numbers, double
    threshold)` to solve the following problem:
Check if in given list of numbers, are any two numbers closer to each other than given
    threshold.
>>> hasCloseElements(Arrays.asList(1.0, 2.0, 3.0), 0.5)
false
>>> hasCloseElements(Arrays.asList(1.0, 2.8, 3.0, 4.0, 5.0, 2.0), 0.3)
true

import java.util.*;
import java.lang.*;

class Solution {
    /**
    Check if in given list of numbers, are any two numbers closer to each other than given threshold
    >>> hasCloseElements(Arrays.asList(1.0, 2.0, 3.0), 0.5)
    false
    >>> hasCloseElements(Arrays.asList(1.0, 2.8, 3.0, 4.0, 5.0, 2.0), 0.3)
    true
    */
    public boolean hasCloseElements(List<Double> numbers, double threshold) {

```

Figure 9: Instruct prompt example

Figure 9 shows an *instruct*-style prompt. This is the instruct version of the same *continue* prompt shown in Figure 8. The instruct prompt contains the same method signature for code generation as the continue prompt. The difference is that, in addition to nesting the implementation instructions in the comment block, the same instructions are also included as raw text at the start of the prompt. Although this is not the case with all examples of instruct prompts in HumanEvalPack-Synthesize, in this example, the language (Java) is specified.

The main difference between the two prompt styles is that the code generation instruction is explicitly stated in the *instruct* prompt. The instruction is repeated and is included in raw text form. This may make the instruction clearer to the model's understanding. As shown in Figure 13 below, a training prompt, generated by the Gemini LLM as a C++ code sample for fine-tuning, contains a textual description of the prompt - not a description embedded in a C++ comment block. Analyzing these differences in prompt formats can inform an improved understanding of the variance in results between benchmark execution runs for the two prompt styles.

3.4 Data Sources and Fine Tuning

This section focuses on the methods employed in this praxis for fine-tuning small language models to improve their performance on specialized code generation tasks, and includes details about the data sources that were used for fine-tuning. Section 3.4.1 Fine-Tuning Overview presents an overview of the fine-tuning technologies and approaches that were used. Section 3.4.2 Agentic Fine-Tuning defines how agentic fine-tuning is used to refocus the capabilities of a model in a specialized area. Section 3.4.3 Agentic Data Sources provides details about the two code data sets that resulted from the agentic fine-tuning process. Section 3.4.4 Public and Hybrid Data Sources describes public datasets that were also for experimental fine-tuning of Phi-3 for this praxis. These datasets are considered in terms of their effectiveness in achieving code generation improvements, compared to model performance achieved through the agentic fine-tuning approach.

3.4.1 Fine-Tuning Overview

Fine-tuning small language models is the fundamental method employed in this praxis to achieve improvements in code generation performance in C++ and Rust. A primary development focus for the praxis was creation of an agentic fine-tuning process for Phi-3, coordinated by Python scripts. Using these tools, one may specify options and parameters for the fine-tuning process.

The Parameter-Efficient Fine Tuning (PEFT) library is used to optimize the running time of the fine-tuning process. To support execution in lower-resourced GPUs on PCs and other edge devices, the *brain floating point* a.k.a. *bfloat16* datatype is used for parameter weight storage. This reduces the amount of required GPU RAM at generation time with the fine-tuned models. The LoRA – Low-Rank Adaptation of Language Models technique is used for optimization. The library implementing this approach "freezes the pre-trained model weights and injects trainable rank decomposition matrices into each layer of the Transformer architecture, greatly reducing the number of trainable parameters for downstream tasks." (Hu et al., 2022, p1) The following layers in the Phi-3-small model are replaced with LoRA layers in the fine-tune: *k_proj, q_proj, v_proj, o_proj, gate_proj, down_proj* and *up_proj*.

The PyTorch library is used for low-level ML functions during the fine-tuning process. The Transformers library is used to support loading and saving models in a standard format – including customized python in the model and the tokenizer. The HuggingFace Datasets library is employed for loading fine-tuning datasets using a standard persistence format and API.

Several key training parameters can be specified on the command line to control operation of the fine-tuning script. These include the training size parameter, which is the number of samples from the training dataset to use for fine-tuning. The batch size for training and evaluation can be specified. These options control how many samples are loaded into GPU RAM for training in each batch, and are essential for limiting GPU RAM utilization, to avoid *out of memory* errors.

Two training modes were implemented: chat-formatted instruction tuning and raw pretraining. The majority of the fine-tunes were performed using chat formatting. The script also supports specifying the number of training epochs – which is the total number of passes through the full dataset that are used to for the fine-tuning job. The script supports early stopping – where the training will halt if a configured number of training steps are executed without an improvement in the evaluation loss.

The training script uses the Transformers library to load the model weights and the tokenizer. To support the ChatML instruction tuning procedure, the dataset is loaded and then a custom mapping function selects fields from the data samples to constitute each training instance. This supports mapping data fields to the *user* and *assistant* ChatML fields, respectively. Once the data has been mapped, the Phi-3 tokenizer is used to map the chat fields to the specific chat tokens that are part of the model architecture. This enables the model to understand the user – assistant structure during fine tuning. The fulldataset is converted into tokens by the Phi-3 tokenizer, using the Transformers and PyTorch libraries.

Another python library from HuggingFace, Transformer Reinforcement Learning (TRL) is used to support Supervised Fine Tuning (SFT) in our Phi-3 fine-tuning script. This library is integrated with the PEFT and LoRA functions mentioned above.

Once fine-tuning has completed according to the specified tuning parameters, the fine-tuned model is saved in the form of a model adapter. Such an adapter contains only the changed model weights – avoiding the need to save the full model, which is large. The fine-tuning script also supports merging the adapter with the full model if needed. Early in the praxis effort, proof-of-concept fine-tunes were performed using the Mistral 7b model, following a similar procedure. The fine-tuning script is derived from fine-tuning examples for Phi-3 from the Phi Cookbook (Phi cookbook).

3.4.2 Agentic Fine-Tuning

The process used to fine-tune Phi-3 small language model variants is essential to achieving the results presented in this praxis. As described in the Phi-3 technical report, publicly available web data is an important input to the original training process for the base model for learning general knowledge. However, for specialized skills, such as coding in a subset of programming languages, additional training and fine-tuning rounds are necessary, using specialized, filtered datasets. (Abdin et al., 2024, p1) The most successful fine-tuning approach employed in this praxis is agentic. "Agent fine-tuning offers an alternative by enabling LLMs to internalize procedural reasoning and domain-specific knowledge through training on relevant data and demonstration trajectories." (Xue et al., 2025, p1). As the results in Chapter 4 show, the fine-tuned model variants demonstrating the largest and most consistent increase in generative coding performance were produced using this agentic approach.

The Phi-3 models are instruction-tuned. In this model data samples used for fine-tuning are structured as multiple segments, including a user-generated and a model-generated segment. The segments are demarcated by tags such as <|user|> or <|assistant|>, which indicate the start and end of these data segments. The former is regarded by the model user-generated, and the latter as model-generated. This data tagging approach enables the model to learn in a request to response or prompt to generation format. The instruction-tuning template used by Phi-3 is called ChatML and was originally developed by OpenAI. As shown in Figure 10, in the HumanEvalPack benchmark code a training example is delimited by these tags. Figure 11 shows how a prompt and a code generation output are represented in a structured data code generation training sample – which is a prompt and code response to solve a coding problem in the sorting domain.

```
prompt = f'<|system|>\n<|end|>\n<|user|>\n{inp}<|end|>\n<|assistant|>\n{prompt_base}'
```

Figure 10: HumanEvalPack chat template

```
<|user|>\\nCreate an algorithm in Python to sort an array of numbers.\\n Input: [9, 3, 5, 1, 6]<|end|>\\n<|assistant|>\\ndef sortArray(arr):\\n
for i in range(len(arr)):\\n    for j in range(i+1,len(arr)):\\n    if arr[i] > arr[j]:\\n    temp = arr[i]\\n    arr[i] = arr[j]\\n
arr[j] = temp\\n    return arr\\n\\narr = [9, 3, 5, 1, 6]\\nprint(sortArray(arr))<|end|>\\n<|endoftext|>
```

Figure 11: ChatML formatted code generation instruction

This chat-formatted instruction tuning approach in the off-the-shelf model has been shown to be effective, based on the high performance of Phi-3 on standard code generation benchmarks like HumanEval. But it presents a challenge when assembling a fine-tuning dataset. Many of the common public datasets for code generation training consist only of code samples and other metadata. For a code generation fine-tuning scenario, such code samples are appropriate for the *assistant* segment of the training instance - but not for the *user* segment. For example, one dataset used in this praxis is *github-code-clean.* This dataset includes over 1 terabyte of code data in 32 programming languages. In this dataset there is no summary field that fits the *user* role in the ChatML formatted instruction-tuning approach.

Data Fields

Field	Type	Description
code	string	content of source file
repo_name	string	name of the GitHub repository
path	string	path of file in GitHub repository
language	string	programming language as inferred by extension
license	string	license of GitHub repository
size	int	size of source file in bytes

Figure 12: Data fields in github-code-clean. Reprinted from (https://huggingface.co/datasets/codeparrot/github-code)

The most effective approach for fine-tuning that significantly improves code generation accuracy in C++ and Rust, as shown by the praxis results, employs an agentic training loop. This approach shows a strong improvement in C++ and Rust generation for both *instruct* and *continue* prompts in the HumanEvalPack-Synthesize benchmark – as shown in Chapter 4—Results and Discussion.

Gemini 2.0 Flash is an LLM with a 1 million token input length and 8,000 token output length. The Gemini 2.0 models are likely sparse mixture of expert (MoE) models, and the parameter count for the models is not disclosed (due to their proprietary status). The Gemini family of models scores highly on coding benchmarks such as LiveCodeBench. (Comanici et al., 2025). This LLM plays the agent role in the agentic fine-tuning process that was developed for this praxis. A commercial, cloud-hosted LLM such as Gemini can be employed using two strategies that are supported by the APIs in the Google cloud platform – interactive and batch-oriented.

In both cases Python scripts coordinate the fine-tuning process, issuing commands to the LLM agent, and fine-tuning the SLM. In the interactive approach, a single code generation prompt is created, and then immediately submitted to the API for generation. The resulting code sample is then added to the dataset. This procedure is then executed in a loop, until a sufficiently large dataset has been produced. Either the partial or full dataset can then be used to fine-tune the model. This approach has the disadvantage of long running times, due to the serial (non-parallel) API execution of commands.

In the batch approach, the coordination script pre-computes all the training prompts in advance. This full batch of prompt is then submitted to the model for generation. The cloud LLM generates the batch of results, which has the advantage of a faster running time per generated sample. The full batch of training samples is then used to fine-tune the model. The batch process for agentic training consists of eight steps. These steps are executed by the agentic coordination scripts.

1. Create a set of prompts for code generation in a target language. To encourage variability in the output, and reduce duplication, the same base prompt is used for all generation prompts, but the content is probabilistically varied. The base prompt used for C++ is: *Devise and solve a coding challenge problem. The goal is to design an interesting problem that lends itself well to a C++ solution. The problem should be similar to a programming interview question for a Software Development Engineer position. Return a JSON object containing the problem description in English, and the solution in syntactically correct C++. Adhere strictly to the given JSON schema. Use a high degree of randomness when generating the solution, to avoid duplicates. Use these model options:*

   temperature = 1.5, top_p = 0.9

2. A set of programming problem domains is provided. This set contains: Arrays, Strings, Linked Lists, Stacks, Queues, Trees, Graphs, Bit Manipulation, Math, Logic Puzzles, Sorting, Searching, Testing, Cryptography, Networking, Concurrency, Threads, Locks, Dynamic Programming, and Recursion. Scores are heuristically assigned to each domain to control output frequency. For 50% of the total generation prompts, a problem domain is inserted, based on the scores. For the remaining 50% of prompts, no domain is specified.
3. Provide a JSON response schema as part of the prompt, such as: *"type": "OBJECT", "properties": { "description": {"type": "STRING"}, "solution": {"type": "STRING"} }, "required": ["description", "solution"]* This schema tells the model to respond with generations than conform to the specified JSON schema - so that the description (the *assistant* section of the sample) and the solution (the *user* section of the sample) can be extracted.
4. Use the Google Cloud Vertex API (https://cloud.google.com/vertex-ai/docs/reference/rest) to batch-generate 150,000 code data samples using this set of prompts.
5. Retrieve the generated data from the Google cloud storage bucket once the generation has completed.
6. Parse the JSONL results generated by Gemini 2.0 Flash. Perform data cleaning to fix any malformed JSON.
7. Convert the resulting dataset to the HuggingFace Datasets format and save it locally.
8. Fine-tune the model using the dataset.

For step 8, the tuning script uses the PyTorch and Transformers python libraries to tune the model using a single Nvidia GPU (GH200). The results documented in Chapter 4—Results and Discussion show the improvements in code generation performance for C++ and Rust, using this fine-tuning process.

3.4.3 Agentic Data Sources

An agentic process was employed to generate two data sets for this praxis, as described in the previous section. Both data sets are structured to include two fields, *prompt* and *code*, in each sample. The *prompt* field consists of an English language prompt for a code generation task. The *code* field is a coding sample in either C++ or Rust, respectively, that implements the specified task.

During the fine-tuning process, each of these data sets was used to create the C++ and Rust specialized Phi-3 coding models. For each sample, the *prompt* field is mapped to the *user* role in the ChatML template. The *code* field is mapped to the *assistant* role. This enables the dataset to be used appropriately during fine-tuning to match the instruction-tuned format of the Phi-3-small model.

The first data set, *agentic-cpp-150k,* consists of 150,000 training samples and is 564 megabytes in size. The second data set, *agentic-rust-150k,* also consists of 150,000 training samples and is 651 megabytes in size. Figure 13 shows a coding prompt from the *agentic-cpp-150k* dataset, where a task is defined to find the k pairs of instances that are closest in length, from an input vector of structs. Figure 14 shows a solution to this problem, which is the corresponding *code* field from the same data sample in the *agentic-cpp-150k* dataset.

```
You are given a list of `n` song durations (in seconds) represented as integers.  Each song is represented by a structure Song { int length; string title; }. You are also given a target duration `k` (in seconds). Your task is to find, for each song, whether there exists another song in the list such that the combined duration of the two songs is as close as possible to `k` without exceeding it. More formally, find the pairing of two songs (distinct indices `i` and `j`) such that `songs[i].length + songs[j].length <= k`, and `songs[i].length + songs[j].length` is maximized. For each song indexed `i` return the song title of the 'partner' song that maximizes the song duration. If no such pair exists for song `i`, return an empty string. Assume the `song` array does not contain duplicates song titles. The song lengths are also unique. For example, if `songs = [{300, "SongA"}, {200, "SongB"}, {150, "SongC"}, {400, "SongD"}]` and `k = 550`, the output should be `["SongB", "SongA", "", "SongA"]`. For SongA, the best pair is SongB (300 + 200 = 500). For SongB, the best pair is SongA (200+300=500). For SongC, no song can be found. For SongD, the best pair is SongA (400 + 300 = 700 > 550, therefore return "SongA" with 400+300=700<=550. The function should return a `std::vector<std::string>`.
```

Figure 13: C++ coding prompt from the agentic-cpp-150k dataset

~~~
```cpp
#include <iostream>
#include <vector>
#include <algorithm>
#include <limits>

using namespace std;

struct Song {
    int length;
    string title;
};

vector<string> findClosestPairs(vector<Song>& songs, int k) {
    int n = songs.size();
    vector<string> result(n, "");

    for (int i = 0; i < n; ++i) {
        int bestMatch = -1;
        int bestSum = numeric_limits<int>::min();

        for (int j = 0; j < n; ++j) {
            if (i != j) {
                int sum = songs[i].length + songs[j].length;
                if (sum <= k && sum > bestSum) {
                    bestSum = sum;
                    bestMatch = j;
                }
            }
        }

        if (bestMatch != -1) {
            result[i] = songs[bestMatch].title;
        }
    }

    return result;
}
~~~

Figure 14: C++ code sample from agentic-cpp-150k dataset

3.4.4 Public and Hybrid Data Sources

The C++ and Rust results demonstrate that for an SLM such as Phi-3, an agentic fine-tuning approach is effective in fine-tuning for code generation in one language. This praxis also touches on alternative approaches to dataset creation, which proved less effective. Several data preprocessing and fine-tuning iterations were performed on the *github-code-clean* dataset. This dataset consists of 111 million code examples in 30 languages – including 19 million Java samples, 321,000 Rust samples and 7.3 million C++ samples. As a pre-processing step, the dataset was filtered for these languages. Many of the fine-tunes shown in the figure are for the Java language, using random subsets of github-code-clean Java samples of varying sizes.

The *Phi-3-small-128k-instruct-finetune-j150k-sum* dataset consists of 150,000 examples of Java source code from the github-code-clean dataset – randomly selected by shuffling the source dataset, using a pseudo-random number generator. To match the required {user, assistant} instruction-tuning chat format needed for fine-tuning, Gemini 2.0-flash was used to generate a summary for each code sample. As in the agentic fine-tuning approach, the Google Vertex API was used for batch generation, with this straightforward prompt: *Summarize this Java code*. To apply the dataset fields to the instruction-tuning chat format, the generation prompt was used along with the original code for the *user* field, and the generated summary was used for the *assistant* response.

Additional fine-tuning datasets were produced and fine-tuning was performed for the CodeComplex dataset (CodeComplex, n.d.). This is a much smaller dataset, with 14,000

Java-only code samples. These samples are rated by runtime complexity, such as *linear* or *quadratic*, and the problems are sourced from coding contest websites like CodeForces (CodeForces, n.d.). We followed a similar hybrid approach as with github-code-clean, using the prompt *Summarize this Java code* to generate summaries of each of the 14,000 instances, using Gemini 2.0-flash. During finetuning, to apply the instruction-tuning chat format to the dataset fields, we used this generation prompt along with the original code, for the *user* field, and the generated summary from Gemini for the *assistant* response.

The remaining datasets produced for this research are from the code-contests dataset. This dataset is also constructed from coding competition data that was sourced from multiple websites. This data was parsed this to extract Java-only code results from arrays of results for individual coding problems – assembling a dataset that contains the original problem formulation, including input / output examples, and the Java solution. In the chat format for this dataset, the *user* segment consists of the coding problem, and the *assistant* segment contains the coding solution, in Java. The results for this fine-tune, labeled as *Phi-3-small-128k-instruct-finetune-code-contests-150k*, show a similar pattern to the other results – a strong improvement from off-the-shelf on the *instruct* prompt, and a significant performance decrease for the *continue* prompt.

3.5 Ensemble Architecture

To support the ultimate praxis objective of enhancing code generation performance for multiple languages and validating such performance increases using benchmarking tools including *bigcode-evaluation-harness* and *humanevalpack-synthesize*, a constraint is the design limitations of the Transformers and PyTorch libraries. A goal of the praxis is to create a drop-in library replacement for the typical single-model pattern supported by deep learning support libraries such as PyTorch. In such libraries, which support a wide range of model implementations yet implement this support using a simple API, there are at least two primary tasks that the library must implement to support AI generative use cases. First, an appropriate tokenizer must be instantiated, that supports input like natural language or program code and generates vectors of output tokens that are compatible with the target library. Second, the model weights and layers must be loaded into the GPU memory. Once those two steps are accomplished, the model and library are ready to execute generation in response to input prompts.

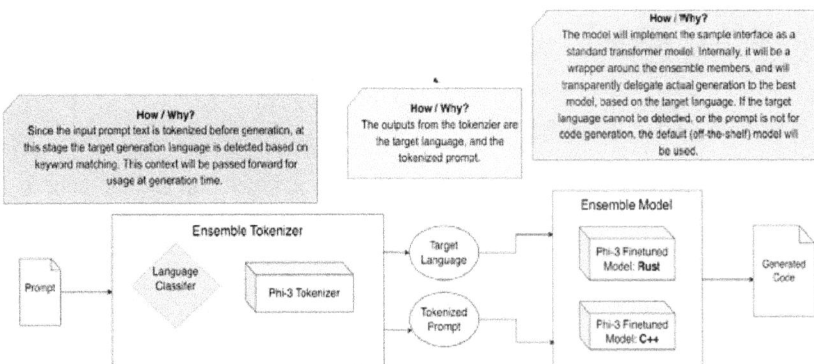

Figure 15: Multi-language AI coding ensemble architecture

Once multiple fine-tuned coding model variants have been created through agentic fine-tuning, the next task is to combine the two models together into an ensemble. As described in Section 2.4 Ensembles of Language Models, there are two high-level categories of ensemble models: architectural-level and model-level ensembles. In architectural approaches, like weight merging or mixture of experts, a single model is created that contains useful knowledge from one or more source models. In model-level approaches, like routing and cascading, instead of combining models together in terms of their layers and weights, a component is added to the model execution system that enables an informed choice to be made at inference time, to choose an optimal model that is expected to perform the best at a given task.

In this praxis, where fine-tuned multiple models have been shown to outperform an off-the-shelf model for code-generation applications, the router-based approach is the most appropriate choice. Figure 15 shows the router-based ensemble architecture. A language classifier has been added into the tokenizer code. This classifier is implemented using keyword matching – not using a neural network. As shown in the figure, the language detection needs to occur during tokenization. This is required because the natural language text of the prompt must be scanned to detect keywords that indicate one language versus another.

Code completion prompts in the *continue* style include the name of the target generation language, such as *C++*. Other keywords are used to detect a language request – such as the *#include* or *using namespace* reserved words for C++. For *instruct* prompts, as shown in Figure 9, the natural language text of the prompt doesn't contain the language name, and so the detection relies on other relevant keywords. A similar approach is used to detect keywords for Rust. If the keyword matching approach is positive for one of the supported languages, then a JSON record of the language choice is saved in local context. If a coding language choice is not detected, the JSON record indicates that the default (off-the-shelf) model should be used for generation.

The next execution stage in the benchmark framework is the generation stage. The *generate* function in the ensemble model has been updated to look for the saved JSON context that has keeps track of the language choice. If a model change action is required, meaning that the current generation task requires a change to a different model, additional code added to the generate function detects this situation, and dynamically loads the required fine-tuned model adapter. That model is that used to perform the generation. This process then continues through successive generation actions. In a coding scenario, a developer may often continue to use a single language, so model changes are infrequent. In cases where the model much be frequently changed, the additional latency introduced by the model change may become a factor.

A distinct advantage of this approach is that, although the Transformers and PyTorch libraries don't natively support ensemble models, our router-based coding SLM ensemble is a drop-in replacement for an ordinary non-ensemble model. This means that the ensemble model developed for this project can be seamlessly used in any AI application that uses standard HuggingFace transformer models, without requiring any other code changes.

3.6 Conclusion

This chapter has presented an in-depth description of the language models, programming languages, procedures and tools used for measurement and evaluation in this research effort. It has also detailed the role of prompting, the data sources used, the fine-tuning method, the architecture and concepts in the SLM ensemble - providing an in-depth treatment of the research methodology.

The development of two fine-tuned variants of the Phi-3 SLM - respectively showing measurable improvements in C++ and Rust coding has been delineated. It has been shown that *HumanEvalPack* is an appropriate benchmark suite for evaluating experimental results from AI code generation methods, due to its pedigree as a multi-language descendant of the standard *HumanEval* coding benchmark, that incorporates the robust *pass@k* metric for measurement of code generation accuracy performance. This chapter has provided a thorough description of a series of fine-tuning experiments with diverse datasets.

The experimental results presented in the next chapter will show that an instruction-tuned SLM such as Phi-3 benefits from an agentic fine-tuning regimen. Observing the impact of the prompt style (*instruct* vs *continue*) on the experimental results supports an agentic fine-tuning approach that addresses multiple prompt formats. Details have been provided showing how the customized fine-tuning process operates. Finally, the ensemble architecture has been documented, showing how it unifies the multi-language fine-tunes in a single container. Notably, the ensemble is a drop-in replacement for AI applications using the standard Transformers library from HuggingFace – which makes the ensemble approach generic and reusable in a broad range of AI software applications.

Chapter 4
Results and Discussion

4.1 Hypobook Testing

As described in Chapter 3, the *bigcode-evaluation-harness* is employed to drive the code generation benchmarking process and save results from the execution of unit tests - in JavaScript Object Notation (JSON) format. Each execution of the *humanevalpack-synthesize* test suite produces the set of output files shown in Table 1.

File	Purpose
logs.json	Tracks pass / fail result for each task and completion. For failures, includes output showing the cause.
references_humanevalsynthesize-<lang>.json	Saves all the unit tests for each task, in the target language (where <lang> is the language generated, such as C++ or Rust)
generations_humanevalsynthesize-<lang>.json	Saves all generated code, for all samples for each task.
evaluation_results.json	Saves the pass@k results for the full benchmark run, and all test parameters.

Table 1: Bigcode-evaluation-harness Benchmark Outputs

To evaluate the experimental benchmark results with respect to the research hypotheses, the McNemar statistical test is employed. This test is a standard tool for evaluating those results that take the form of a dichotomous variable. The *humanevalpack-synthesize* results are produced in this form. For the set of generations produced for each test, each result is recorded as a *pass / fail.* This result tracks the successful or unsuccessful execution of the unit test.

"The McNemar test (1947) is best described as a 2x2 cross classification of paired (or matched) responses to a dichotomous item. In simple terms, the McNemar test can be viewed as a type of chi-square test that uses dependent (i.e., correlated or paired) data rather than independent (unrelated) samples." (Adedokun & Burgess, 2012, p126) "The McNemar test is a non-parametric statistical test; i.e., it is distribution free and can be used with data sets and samples that are not normally distributed." (Ciechalski, Pinkney, & Weaver, 2002) (Adedokun & Burgess, 2012, p126) Since there is no guarantee that the test outputs from *humanevalpack-synthesize* are normally distributed, the McNemar Test is a more appropriate choice for these data than other tests that make that assumption – such as a paired sample t-test.

For these experimental results, each dichotomous result is dependent – since it is pair of results for a given test and generation. For each experimental run, all pass / fail unit test results from the benchmark are loaded from a benchmark output file and then organized as shown in Table 2. This table is referred to as a contingency table or classification table. The table captures the changes in corresponding pairs of results, in two runs of the experimental benchmark. The first run is the benchmark result set from the base model, and the second run is the benchmark result set from the fine-tuned model. All values in the table are in the form of counts. The count in the lower-left corner shows how many failures in the base run changed to passes in the fine-tune run. This is of particular interest as it captures the improvement in the fine-tuned model. The count in upper-right corner shows how many passes in the base run changed to fails in the fine-tune run. This is also a notable measurement since it captures regressions in generative

	Fine-Tuned Model: Pass (1)	**Fine-Tuned Model: Fail (0)**
Base Model: Pass (1)	*Both Pass (count)*	*Base Pass, Fine-Tune Fail (count)*
Base Model: Fail (0)	*Base Fail, Fine-Tune Pass (count)*	*Both Fail (count)*

Table 2: Sample Contingency Table (McNemar)

capability – showing the number of tests that failed with the fine-tuned model, having succeeded with the base model.

The sample contingency table shown is similar in form to a confusion matrix but differs in that it compares benchmark results (pass / fail) for two models. Here, results from a fine-tuned model and a base model are compared. In contrast, a confusion matrix is often used to compare classification predictions from a single model versus ground truth classifications.

4.2 Code Generation

This section presents the relevant results generated during experiments. These experiments focus on improvements in the fine-tuned specialist code generation models, and the ensemble of fine-tuned models, in comparison with the code generation performance of the base model. The procedure for generation is described in Section 3.3 Measurement and Evaluation. As discussed in Section 2.2.1 Code Generation Using Small Language Models, the focus of this research is two related problems: code completion and code generation. The prompt type configuration option for code completion in *bigcode-evaluation-harness* is *continue* and the option for code generation is *instruct*. This naming convention is used in these tables of results.

4.2.1 Code Generation: Rust

This subsection presents the experimental results for the Rust language. Results are presented in the contingency table format, and include pass@10 statistics and statistics from the McNamer's hypobook test. The tables contrast the results from the base model and the fine-tuned model, for Rust. Results are shown for both prompt styles (continue and instruct) individually, and also in a single combined table for both styles.

Rust Language - Prompt Style: Continue		
	Fine-Tuned Model (Rust): Pass (1)	**Fine-Tuned Model (Rust): Fail (0)**
Base Model: Pass (1)	517	160
Base Model: Fail (0)	567	2036
p-value	3.07E-51	
x^2 statistic	226.73	
pass@10 (base)	36.51	
pass@10 (fine-tuned)	47.14	
pass@10 (delta)	10.63	

Table 3: Test Results - Rust Fine-Tune, Continue Prompt

Table 3 shows the benchmark performance on *humanevalpack-synthesize* for the Rust language, for the *continue* prompt style (code completion). The experiment is a comparison of the results for the Phi-3 base model and the model produced during this research effort, which was fine-tuned using the *synth-rust-150k* dataset.

The contingency table shows the changes in the paired results for the base model and fine-tuned model. The pairs measured here are unit test results in corresponding ordered positions in the result set, for the two sets of results. The contingency table is similar in form to a confusion matrix but differs in that it compares benchmark results (binary pass / fail) for two models. In this case, results from a fine-tuned model and a base model are compared. In contrast, a confusion matrix typically compares classification predictions from a single model with ground truth classifications.

There are 164 prompts and corresponding unit tests in the *humanevalpack-synthesize* test suite. The test harness is configured to produce 20 samples per prompt – resulting in

3280 pass / fail results (n = 3280). Therefore, the sum of the four pass / fail comparison counts in the contingency table is also 3280.

Rust Language - Prompt Style: Instruct		
	Fine-Tuned Model (Rust): Pass (1)	**Fine-Tuned Model (Rust): Fail (0)**
Base Model: Pass (1)	409	171
Base Model: Fail (0)	877	1823
p-value	3.79E-105	
x^2 statistic	474.26	
pass@10 (base)	36.28	
pass@10 (fine-tuned)	54.4	
pass@10 (delta)	18.12	

Table 4: Test Results - Rust Fine-Tune, Instruct Prompt

The counts in the upper-left and lower-right, 517 and 2036 respectively, show that the base model results have a much higher failure rate. The table shows that the improvement count (567, lower left) is high – greater than the number of generations that continued to pass (upper left, 517). The *pass@10* statistics reflect the same pattern. The positive delta greater than 10 also reflects the large improvement count, and comparatively small regression count.

The lower-left count – 567 transitions from fail in the base model to pass in the fine-tuned model – demonstrate that the fine-tuning procedure showed a high level of success in improving the model performance. The count in the upper-right (160), showing transitions from pass in the base model to fail in the fine-tuned model, shows that while there is a measurable regression in certain paired samples, the improvement in the fine-tune is much greater than the regression amount. This is a positive result suggesting significant improvement – which is also reflected in the p-value. The p-value, measuring the likelihood of incorrectly rejecting the null hypobook, is very close to zero, at 3.07e-51. Compared to the standard α of 0.05, this very low p-value supports statistically significant improvement in the Rust generative coding performance for the continue prompt style. This significant improvement is also supported by the 18.12 positive delta in the *pass@10* score.

The results in Table 4 show the code generation benchmark performance on *humanevalpack- synthesize* for the Rust language, for the *instruct* prompt style. The benchmark was executed on the same Rust fine-tuned model that was used for the *continue* results described above and shown in Table 3, and the contingency table follows the same format, with the same number of tests and samples.

The *instruct* results for Rust show a similar pattern as the *continue* results. The transition count from fail to pass (877), shown in the lower left of the table, shows an even greater increase in the generative coding capability for this prompt style with the fine-tuned model, compared to the *continue* prompt style. There is a similar pattern shown in the upper-right count, which measures transitions in the fine-tuned benchmark – at 171, the number of regressions measured is far lower than the number of improvements (877). With this number of improvements, a comparison with the Rust *continue* improvement count (567) indicates that when using this model and dataset, the *instruct* prompt results are more conducive to improvement. The p-value, measuring the likelihood of incorrectly rejecting the null hypobook, is very close to zero, at 3.79e-105.

Rust Language - Prompt Style: Combined		
	Fine-Tuned Model (Rust): Pass (1)	**Fine-Tuned Model (Rust): Fail (0)**
Base Model: Pass (1)	926	331
Base Model: Fail (0)	1444	3859
p-value	1.60E-153	
x^2 statistic	696.64	
pass@10 (base)	36.395	
pass@10 (fine-tuned)	50.77	
pass@10 (delta)	14.375	

Table 5: Test Results - Rust Fine-Tune, Combined Results

This p-value is substantially lower than the p-value for Rust *continue*. Compared to the standard α of 0.05, this very low p-value supports statistically significant improvement in Rust generative coding performance for the *instruct* prompt style.

Table 5 shows the benchmark performance on *humanevalpack-synthesize* for the Rust language, for both the *continue* and *instruct* prompts styles. The McNemar's input is the same as the previous tests – with 3280 examples each for the two prompt types, for the base model and fine-tuned model. The lists of pass / fail results are concatenated row-major, resulting in 6560 samples. The McNamer's test is performed for this full combined test. The number of improvements in the combined Rust test (lower left) is 1444, and the number of regressions is 331. Since the number of improvements is more than 4x the number of regressions, this demonstrates the strong improvement in code generation by the fine-tuned model. The p-value, measuring the likelihood of incorrectly rejecting the null hypobook, is very close to 0 at 1.60e-153. This shows that a fine-tuned SLM demonstrates statistically significant improvement in the HumanEvalPack benchmark score for coding in Rust, compared to an off-the-shelf SLM. The clear improvement in the *pass@10* score, showing a positive delta of 14.38, provides further evidence for this improvement.

4.2.2 Code Generation: C++

This subsection presents the experimental results for the C++ language. Results are presented in the contingency table format, and include pass@10 statistics and statistics from the McNamer's hypobook test. The tables contrast the results from the base model and the fine-tuned model, for C++. Results are shown for both prompt styles (continue and instruct) individually, and also in a single combined table for both styles.

C++ Language - Prompt Style: Continue		
	Fine-Tuned Model (C++): Pass (1)	**Fine-Tuned Model (C++): Fail (0)**
Base Model: Pass (1)	1180	231
Base Model: Fail (0)	549	1320
p-value	7.38E-30	
x^2 statistic	128.83	
pass@10 (base)	57.59	
pass@10 (fine-tuned)	66.52	
pass@10 (delta)	8.93	

Table 6: Test Results - C++ Fine-Tune, Continue Prompt

Table 6 and Table 7 show the Phi-3 C++ fine- tuning results in contingency table format, compared with the Phi-3 base model – for the *continue* and *instruct* prompt styles, respectively. The *synth-cpp-150k* dataset was used to train the fine-tuned model that produced these results. One notable difference from the Rust results is that the stable pass count is higher before and after fine-tuning, for the same *continue* prompt style - 1180 for C++ vs 517 for Rust. This indicates stronger performance overall for C++ code generation, compared to Rust. For both prompt styles, the improvement count (lower-left) exceeds the regression count (upper-right). This is consistent with the p-values for both sets of measurements (*continue* and *instruct*). For *continue*, the p-value is 7.38e-30, and for *instruct* it is 7.96e-79. Both p-values are very close to zero, strongly supporting significant performance based on the standard α of 0.05. For the *continue* prompt style, the positive delta for the *pass@10* metric is 8.93. For the *instruct* prompt style, the positive delta for *pass@10* is 9.55. These metric results also support a strong improvement – although not as great an improvement as seen in the corresponding results for the Rust language.

C++ Language - Prompt Style: Instruct			
	Fine-Tuned Model (C++): Pass (1)		**Fine-Tuned Model (C++): Fail (0)**
Base Model: Pass (1)		1256	133
Base Model: Fail (0)		665	1226
p-value	7.96E-79		
x^2 statistic	353.33		
pass@10 (base)		57.18	
pass@10 (fine-tuned)		66.73	
pass@10 (delta)		9.55	

Table 7: Test Results - C++ Fine-Tune, Instruct Prompt

Table 8 presents the results for C++ code generation benchmark performance on *humanevalpack-synthesize*, in a combined format that measures both *continue* and *instruct* prompt styles. Following the same procedure as the Rust benchmark performance, the McNemar's input is the same as the previous tests – with 3280 examples each for the two prompt types, for the base model and fine-tuned model. These lists of pass / fail results are concatenated row-major, resulting in 6560 samples. The McNamer's test is performed for this full combined test. The number of improvements in the combined C++ test (lower left) is 1214, and the number of regressions is 364. Since the number of improvements is more than 3x the number of regressions, this demonstrates the strong improvement in code generation by the fine-tuned model. The p-value, measuring the likelihood of incorrectly rejecting the null hypobook, is very close to 0 at 2.41e-101. This result supports significant improvement in coding performance for C++. The improvement in the *pass@10* score, with a positive delta of 9.24, provides additional supporting evidence.

C++ Language - Prompt Style: Combined		
	Fine-Tuned Model (C++): Pass (1)	**Fine-Tuned Model (C++): Fail (0)**
Base Model: Pass (1)	2436	364
Base Model: Fail (0)	1214	2546
p-value	2.41E-101	
x^2 statistic	456.78	
pass@10 (base)	57.385	
pass@10 (fine-tuned)	66.625	
pass@10 (delta)	9.24	

Table 8: Test Results - C++ Fine-Tune, Combined Results

Multi-language Ensemble - Prompt Style: Continue		
	Ensemble - C++ and Rust: Pass (1)	**Ensemble - C++ and Rust: Fail (0)**
Base Model: Pass (1)	1679	409
Base Model: Fail (0)	1122	3350
p-value	5.48E-74	
x^2 statistic	331.12	
average pass@10 (base)	47.05	
average pass@10 (ensemble)	57.25	
average pass@10 (delta)	10.2	

Table 9: Test Results - Multi-Language Ensemble, Continue Prompt

Multi-language Ensemble - Prompt Style: Instruct			
		Ensemble - C++ and Rust: Pass (1)	Ensemble - C++ and Rust: Fail (0)
Base Model: Pass (1)		1672	297
Base Model: Fail (0)		1544	3047
p-value	2.08E-185		
x^2 statistic	843.30		
average pass@10 (base)		46.73	
average pass@10 (ensemble)		61	
average pass@10 (delta)		14.27	

Table 10: Test Results - Multi-Language Ensemble, Instruct Prompt

4.2.3 Code Generation: Multi-Language Ensemble

Table 9 and Table 10 present combined results in contingency table format, for multi-language benchmarks of C++ and Rust code generation – which were generated using the router-based ensemble approach developed for this research effort. For these results, a choice is made to use one of the fine-tuned models comprising the ensemble, based on the programming language detected for the prompt.

Once generated, the two sets of pass / fail results for both languages from the ensemble are concatenated together. This results in a total pass / fail result set of 6560 elements. Table 9, containing the results for the *continue* prompt, shows that the improvement count in the lower-left (1122) is far greater than the regression count in the upper-right (409). The two fine-tuned models, considered in tandem for the *continue* prompt format, outperform the base model. In Table 10 containing the results for the *instruct* prompt, the improvement count in the lower-left (1544) is far greater than the regression count in the upper-right (297). This shows that the two fine-tuned models, used in tandem in a router-based ensemble, outperform the base model. This pattern of results is consistent with the individual fine-tuned results shown above. Compared to the standard α of 0.05, the very low p-values of 5.48e-74 (*continue* prompts) and 2.08e-185 (*instruct* prompts) supports statistically significant improvement. The evidence for this improvement is bolstered by the increase of 10.2 in the *pass@10* metric for the *continue* prompt and 14.27 for the *instruct* prompt style.

Multi-language Ensemble - Prompt Style: Combined			
		Ensemble - C++ and Rust: Pass (1)	Ensemble - C++ and Rust: Fail (0)
Base Model: Pass (1)		3351	706
Base Model: Fail (0)		2666	6397
p-value	1.73E-249		
x^2 statistic	1,138.10		
average pass@10 (base)		46.89	
average pass@10 (ensemble)		59.125	
average pass@10 (delta)		12.235	

Table 11: Test Results - Multi-Language Ensemble, Combined Results

Table 11 presents the multi-language code generation benchmark results for C++ and Rust in a combined format that measures both *continue* and *instruct* prompt styles. Following the same method as the other tests, the input to McNemar's is 13,120 examples each for the base model, and the fine-tuned ensemble model. Each of these sets of pass / fail results are concatenated row-major. This is twice the number of samples used in the previous multi-language tests – because the previous tests were partitioned by prompt style.

The number of improvements is 2666, and the number of regressions is 706. Since the number of improvements is more than 3x the number of regressions, this demonstrates the strong improvement in code generation by the ensemble model. The p-value of 1.73e-249, measuring the likelihood of incorrectly rejecting the null hypobook, is extremely close to 0. This result supports significant improvement in code generation capability for the multi-language ensemble. The *pass@10* metric for this benchmark test shows an improvement of 12.24 for the multi-language ensemble, compared to the base model. This supports the strong performance improvement measurement.

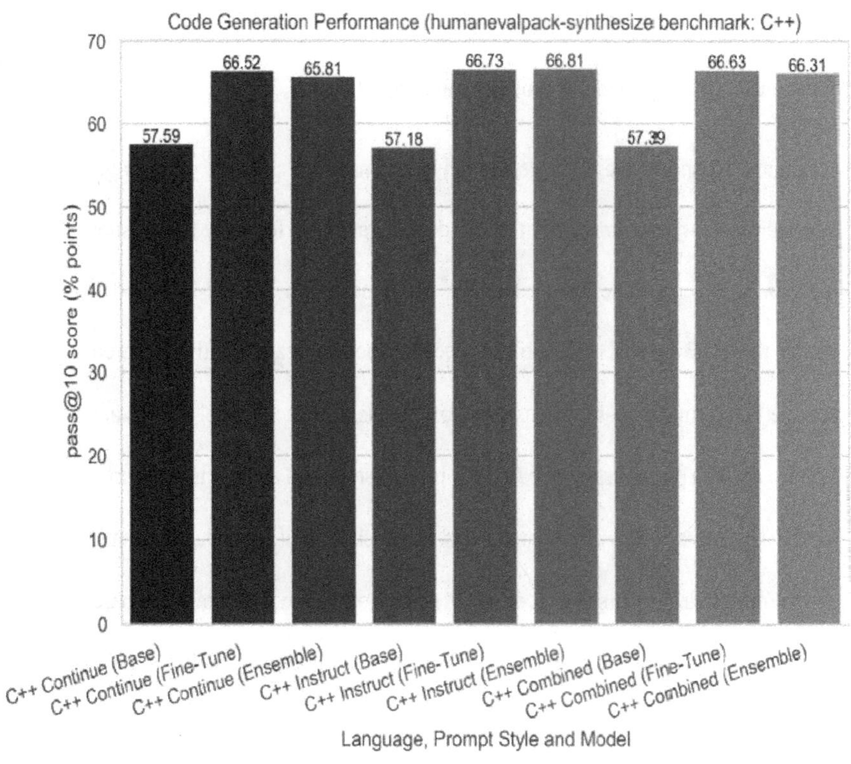

Figure 16: Code Generation Performance - C++

4.3 Code Generation Performance

This section presents bar charts of the pass@10 benchmark results for code generation performance, including all relevant comparisons between results for fine-tuned models and ensemble models. The charts are organized first by language (C++ and Rust), and finally in a multi-language format that pertains to the multi-language ensemble results. The charts highlight the improvements for each language between the off-the-shelf (base) model the fine-tuned models. They also highlight the related improvements between the off-shelf-model and the ensemble model.

Figure 16 shows the code generation performance for the C++ language on the *humanevalpack-synthesize* benchmark. Code generation performance is measured using the *pass@10* score. The chart compares performance on the Phi-3-small-128k base model, the Phi-3 small C++ fine-tuned specialist model (created for this research effort), and the Phi-3-small fine-tuned ensemble of models. For each model, results are shown for the *continue* prompt style, the *instruct* prompt style, and a combined (average) value for the *continue* and *instruct* prompt styles. For each prompt style, the fine-tuned results and the ensemble results show a consistent pattern of improvement over the base model. For each prompt style, the fine-tuned and ensemble results show a delta of less than one percentage point.

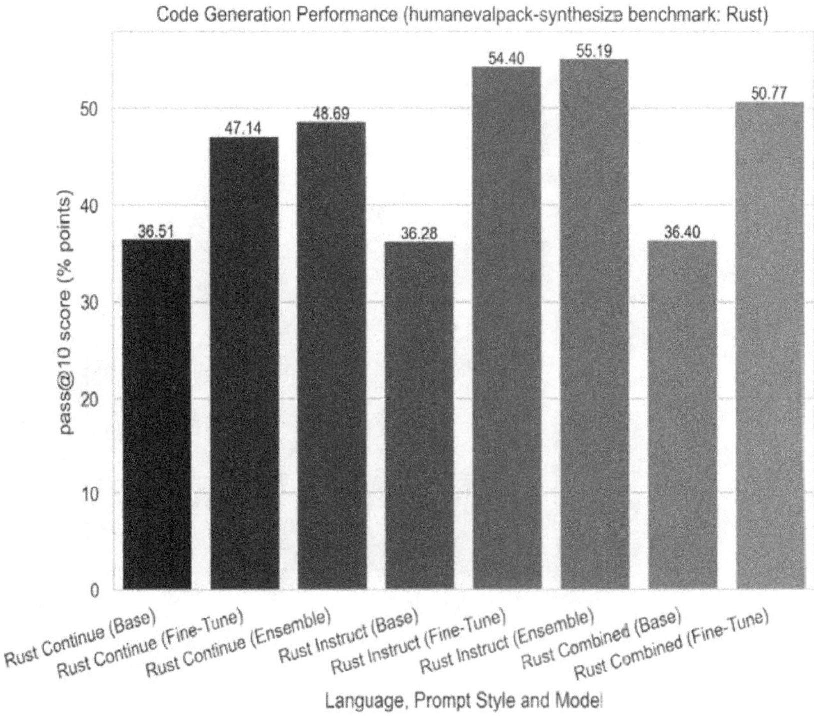

Figure 17: Code Generation Performance - Rust

Figure 17 shows the code generation performance for the Rust language on the *humanevalpack-synthesize* benchmark. Code generation performance is measured by the *pass@10* score. The chart compares performance on the Phi-3-small-128k base model, the Phi-3 small Rust fine-tuned specialist model (created for this research effort), and the Phi-3-small fine-tuned ensemble of models. For each model, results are shown for the *continue* prompt style, the *instruct* prompt style, and a combined (average) value for the *continue* and *instruct* prompt styles. For each prompt style, the fine-tuned results and the ensemble results show a consistent pattern of improvement over the base model. For each prompt style, the ensemble result shows and improvement of about one percentage point, compared to the fine-tuned results.

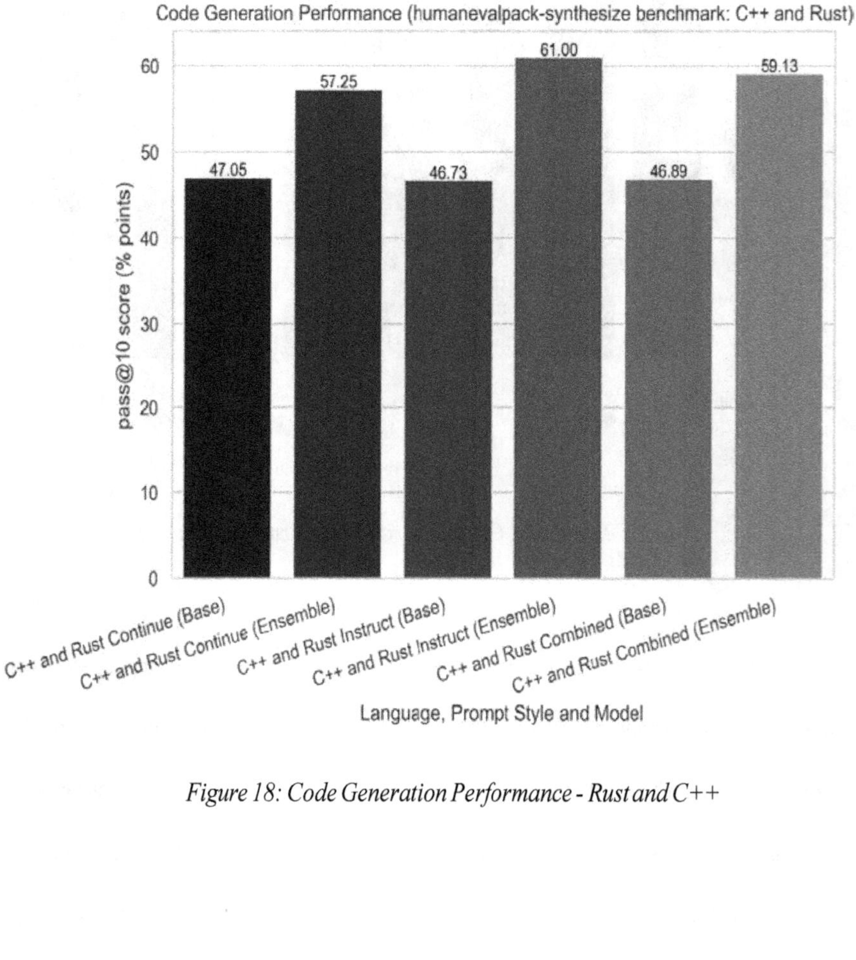

Figure 18: Code Generation Performance - Rust and C++

Figure 18 shows the code generation performance for both the Rust and C++ languages, on the *humanevalpack-synthesize* benchmark. The chart compares performance on the Phi-3-small-128k base model, the Phi-3-small Rust fine-tuned specialist model (created for this research effort), and the Phi-3-small fine-tuned ensemble of models. Code generation performance is measured using the average *pass@10* score for each model and prompt style. For each model, average results for the two languages are shown for the *continue* prompt style, the *instruct* prompt style, and a combined (also an average) value for the *continue* and *instruct* prompt styles. For each prompt style, the fine-tuned results and the ensemble results show a consistent pattern of improvement over the base model. For each prompt style, the ensemble result shows and improvement of about one percentage point, compared to the fine-tuned results.

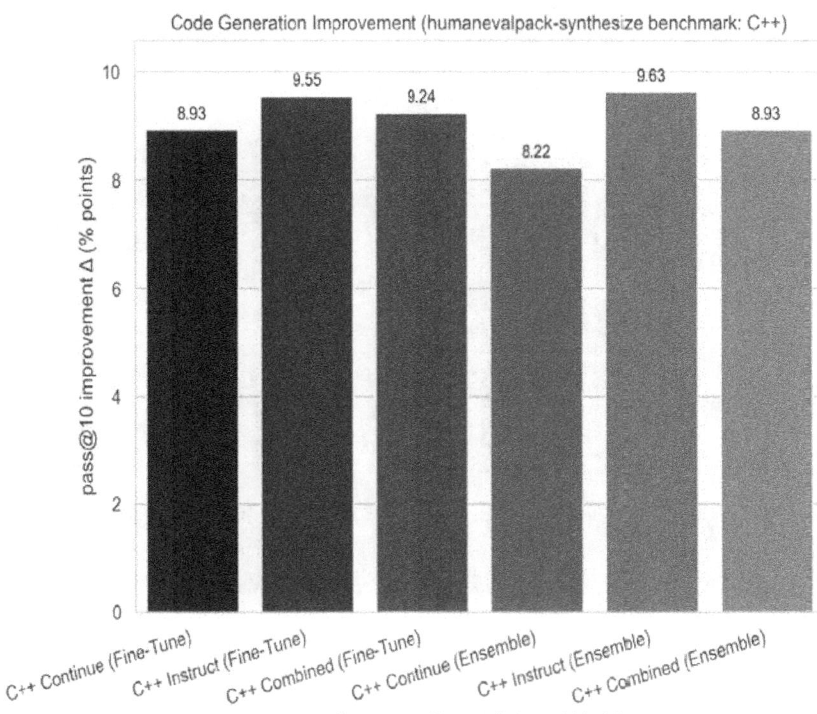

Figure 19: Code Generation Improvement - C++

Error! Reference source not found. summarizes the code generation performance results for C++. Each value in the bar chart is an improvement delta (Δ), in percentage points, for a style of prompt (*continue* and *instruct*), or a combined (average) improvement delta. For each data point, the delta values show the improvement when compared to the Phi-3 base model. For both the C++ fine-tuned model and the ensemble model, there is a slightly greater improvement for the *instruct* prompt style versus the *continue* prompt style. In all cases shown in this chart, the improvement is at least 8 points.

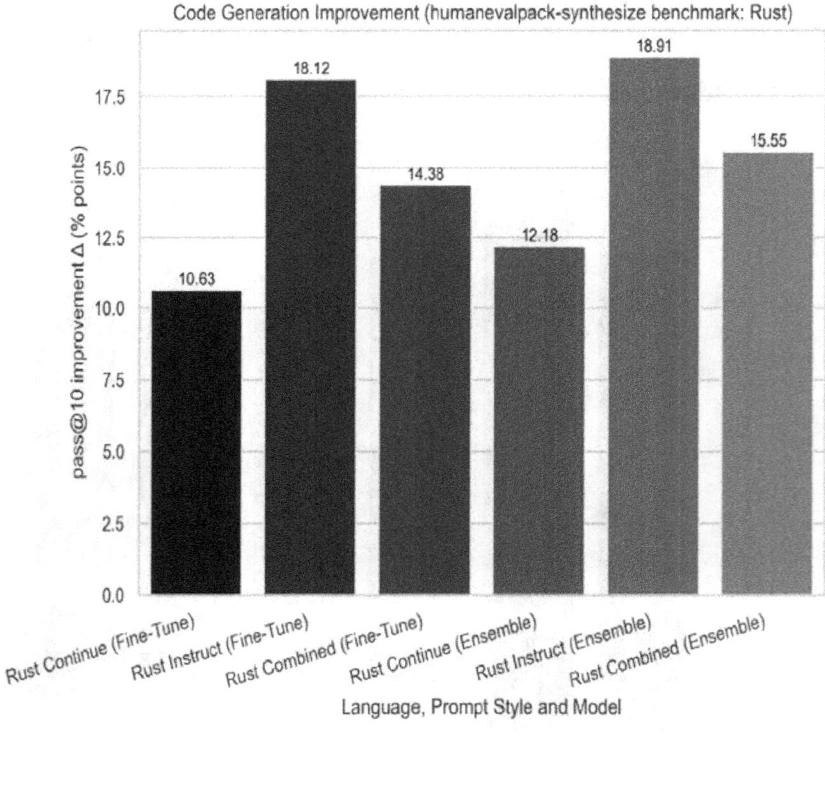

Figure 20: Code Generation Improvement - Rust

Figure 20 summarizes the code generation performance results for Rust. Each value in the bar chart is an improvement delta (Δ), in percentage points, for a style of prompt (*continue* and *instruct*), or a combined (average) improvement delta. For each data point, the delta values show the improvement when compared to the Phi-3 base model. For both the Rust fine-tuned model and the ensemble model, there is a slightly greater improvement for the *instruct* prompt style versus the *continue* prompt style. In all cases shown in this chart, the improvement is at least 10 points. The Rust results show a greater improvement than the C++ results. Similarly to the C++ results, the improvement for *instruct* is more significant than the improvement for *continue* – but to a greater extent for Rust.

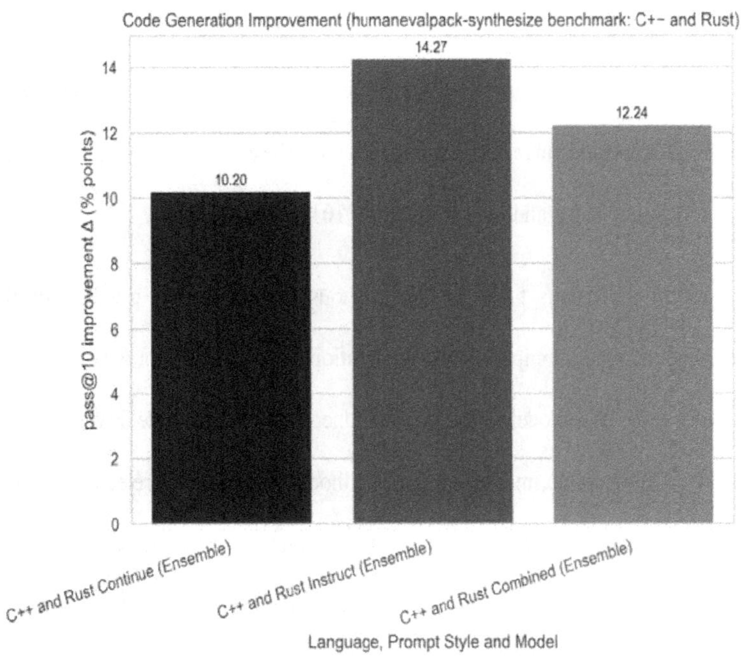

Figure 21: Code Generation Improvement - C++ and Rust

Figure 21 summarizes the code generation performance results for the ensemble model created in this research effort, for multi-language generation in both C++ and Rust. Each value in the bar chart is an improvement delta (Δ), in percentage points, for a style of prompt (*continue* and *instruct*), or a combined (average) improvement delta. For each data point, the delta values show the improvement when compared to the Phi-3 base model. The multi-language results are an average of the results for each language (as measured individually, using the ensemble). As in the single language results, the multi-language results show a greater improvement for the *instruct* prompt style, compared to the *continue* prompt style. In all cases shown in the chart, the improvement is at least 10 points. The combined (average) multi-language improvement is 12.24 percentage points.

4.4 Hypobook Validation

This section focuses on the praxis research questions and research hypotheses and explains how the experimental results support each one. The explanations are provided in the context of hypobook tests and analysis of pass@10 benchmark results.

As shown in the results tables in the previous subsection, the p-value for the McNamer's hypobook test comparing code generation performance improvement for the C++ language for the base model versus the fine-tuned C++ coding model is very close to 0 at 2.41e-101. This p-value, measuring the likelihood of incorrectly rejecting the null hypobook, is far below the standard α of 0.05. **This supports the alternative hypobook for Research Question 1 – that a fine-tuned SLM demonstrates statistically significant improvement in the HumanEvalPack benchmark score for coding in C++, compared to an off-the-shelf SLM.**

The C++ single-model fine-tuned results, compared with off-the-shelf results, also **support Research Hypobook 1** – showing average improvement (considering both prompt styles, *continue* and *instruct*) of 9.24%, exceeding the threshold of 7%.

As shown above, the p-value for the McNamer's hypobook test comparing code generation performance improvement for the Rust language for the base model versus the fine-tuned Rust coding model is very close to 0 at 1.60e-153. This p-value, measuring the likelihood of incorrectly rejecting the null hypobook, is far below the standard α of 0.05. **This supports the alternative hypobook for Research Question 2 – that a fine-tuned SLM demonstrates statistically significant improvement in the HumanEvalPack benchmark score for coding in Rust, compared to an off-the-shelf SLM.**

The Rust single-model fine-tune results, compared with off-the-shelf results, also **support Research Hypobook 2** – showing average improvement (considering both prompt styles, *continue* and *instruct*) of 14.38%, exceeding the threshold of 7%.

As shown above, the p-value for the McNamer's hypobook test comparing multi-language ensemble code generation performance for C++ and Rust, versus the base model, is very close to 0 at 1.73e-249. This p-value, measuring the likelihood of incorrectly rejecting the null hypobook, is far below the standard α of 0.05. **This result supports the alternative hypobook in Research Question 3 – that a fine-tuned SLM ensemble demonstrates statistically significant improvement in the HumanEvalPack benchmark score for coding in both C++ and Rust, compared to an off-the-shelf SLM.**

For the multi-language ensemble model, the average pass@10 improvement of 12.24% (compared to the base model pass@10 score) exceeds the 10% threshold set for

Research Hypobook 3 – supporting this hypobook. This research question connects directly to the book statement for this praxis: that *an ensemble of SLMs fine-tuned on customized code datasets will improve average C++ and Rust code generation accuracy by at least 10% compared to an off-the-shelf SLM - increasing software development productivity*. Since the pass@10 improvement of 12.24% exceeds the threshold of 10%, this result also supports the book statement.

Chapter 5
Conclusions and Future Work

5.1 Conclusions

This chapter provides a summary of the significant findings of this praxis, and shows how these findings support the book statement, that *an ensemble of SLMs fine-tuned on customized code datasets will improve average C++ and Rust code generation accuracy by at least 10% compared to an off-the-shelf SLM - increasing software development productivity.*

The code generation improvement experiments performed for this praxis used the Phi-3-small-128k small language model developed by Microsoft. As shown in detail in Section 4.2 Code Generation, two fine-tuned specialist coding models, one for C++ and another for Rust, were developed by fine-tuning Phi-3 on two customized code datasets. As shown in Table 5, the *pass@10* coding benchmark score for Rust was improved by 14.38 percentage points using the Rust fine-tuned Phi-3 variant. As shown in Table 8, the *pass@10* coding benchmark score for C++ was improved by 9.24 percentage points, using the C++ fine-tuned Phi-3 variant. Using the ensemble model, comprised of both Phi-3 fine-tuned variants (for C++ and Rust), the average *pass@10* score for both languages improved by 12.24 percentage points, as shown in Table 11. These improvements encompass a robust prompting strategy that includes both code completion (*continue*) and code generation (*instruct*) prompt types.

The McNamer's hypobook test results for each of these three scenarios (C++, Rust, and Multi-language ensemble) support acceptance of the alternative hypobook (H1) for the three corresponding research questions, because statistically significant improvement in the HumanEvalPack benchmark scores have been demonstrated for C++, Rust and for a multi-language ensemble that supports both C++ and Rust. This result supports the first part of the book statement, that *an ensemble of SLMs fine-tuned on customized code datasets will improve average C++ and Rust code generation accuracy by at least 10% compared to an off-the-shelf SLM.*

A unique router-based SLM ensemble architecture was created for this project. It includes fine-tuned variant models specialized in code generation for both C++ and Rust and maintains API compatibility with the PyTorch inference API that is typically used for non-ensemble models. As shown in Figure 3, the ensemble model consists of a prompt classifier and a model adapter loader that can dynamically switch the fine-tuned model adapter that is into GPU VRAM. With respect to the standard ensemble model types described in Section 2.4 Ensembles of Language Models, this ensemble is *router-based.*

The fine-tuning procedure described in Section 3.4 Data Sources and Fine Tuning is a key aspect of the research. The Phi-3 model, like many coding AI models, is instruction tuned, meaning that fine-tuning is effective only when data samples conforming to a compatible ChatML format are used. instruction formatted dataset is employed. An LLM, Gemini 2.0, is engaged in the agentic fine-tuning process developed for this praxis, as described in Section 3.4.2 Agentic Fine-Tuning. Fine-tuning the Phi-3 model using advanced techniques including Parameter-Efficient Fine Tuning (PEFT) and Low-Rank Adaptation of Language Models (LoRA) enables code generation accuracy improvements in the fine-tuned models, which was essential to support the research hypotheses for code quality improvement, resulting in developer productivity improvement.

The book statement also encompasses *increasing software development productivity*. As described in Cheng et al. (2022), both objective and subjective measurements may be used to measure productivity. One such measurement, used in (Cheng et al., 2022), consists of productivity self-ranking by developers, on a scale of 1 to 5, where 1 represents a rating of *not productive* and 5 represents rating of *extremely productive*. Development productivity may be considered a function of code quality. An objective measurement of code quality used in (Cheng et al., 2022) is *Median Wall-Clock Merge Time*. This metric represents the actual amount of waiting time between the time when a developer submits a code change for approval, and the time when the code in merged into the code repository. The assumption inherent in this measurement is that higher-quality code will be merged within a shorter time interval, because fewer changes will be needed to meet the bar of sufficient quality for merging into a production code base.

The metrics from *bigcode-evaluation-harness* and the *humanevalpack-synthesize* benchmark suite used in this research provide a yardstick for evaluation that is closely tied to such real-world metrics. In these benchmarks, unit tests in multiple languages, written by human programmers, are executed on the AI-generated code and produce an empirical result. This result consists of pass-fail result counts per unit test, and the *pass@k* metric percentage is computed from these pass-fail results. Therefore, the *pass@k* metric may be considered an indirect measurement of objective software development productivity for Rust and C++ coding, using the fine-tuned specialist coding models for those languages that were created for this effort. Since it utilizes the same fine-tuned models, the ensemble model *pass@k* improvement delta further supports software development productivity improvements for multiple languages.

See Section 3.3 Measurement and Evaluation for further detail on the evaluation methodology, and 4.2 Code Generation for detailed results on the metrics improvements, and hypobook testing which measure the significance of the code quality improvements.

To conclude this praxis, historical context is worthy of consideration in the problem space of automated code generation. One of the fundamental concepts in computer architecture, which has persisted for more than 80 years, is the Von Neumann architecture (Von Neumann, 1945). In this architecture, which is implemented in most modern computers, the CPU is attached via a bus to system memory. Input and output devices are also attached to the CPU. The Von Neumann architecture is an example of a stored-program architecture, where a program is stored in memory before it can be executed.

System memory stores both program code, in the form of machine instructions, and data. For example, for a division operation, the machine instruction for division will be stored in one location in program memory. When the CPU executes the division operation, it computes the results, which consists of the quotient and remainder. These results are stored in another location in memory. Significantly, until the advent of coding AI models and other automated code generation tools, all program code executed on a stored-program computer was first written by a human programmer. With AI coding models, including ensembles of fine-tuned SLMs combined in an ensemble, a stored-program computer can itself create the code that it will execute. This represents a dramatic evolutionary step in the how software is created and executed in a stored-program computer. The research detailed in this praxis provides empirical evidence that the stored-program Von Neumann architecture can be extended to enable computers to write code themselves, based on natural-language prompting by humans, and then execute that code on the same architecture. This may be considered an extension of the concept of Self-Modifying Code (SMC). (Cai, Shao, & Vaynberg, 2007).

5.2 Future Work

The ensemble model architecture described in Section 3.5 Ensemble Architecture supports two fine-tuned model variants of the Phi-3 model: one for the C++ language, and another for Rust. This approach can be scaled to support additional languages, including mainstream languages like Java, or more obscure ones like Erlang or Clojure, by adding additional fine-tuned model variants to the ensemble. The agentic fine-tuning approach outlined in Section 3.4.2 Agentic Fine-Tuning can applied to other languages. Considering the rapid pace of development in commercial LLMs like Gemini, agentic fine-tuning results may improve over time even for less popular languages.

An expected side-effect of supporting additional models in the ensemble is that the prompt classifier may need to detect more subtle variations in the input prompt, when detecting the most appropriate output language. The keyword-matching approach currently used in the classifier could be replaced with a deep learning approach. One implementation challenge for such a classifier would be obtaining enough high-quality training data.

In addition to the fine-tuned model variants in the ensemble, the base Phi-3 model could also be included as an ensemble member. This architectural change would bring the more predictable capabilities of the base model into play in the ensemble. Using the base model would be advantageous in cases where the input prompt is challenging to categorize, with respect to whether it is a coding prompt or not. The base model could also be used for cases where the input prompt is a request to generate code, but the intended target language is not obvious.

The possible applications of SLM ensembles do not end with coding. Fine-tuned SLMs may be created for numerous generative AI domains – such as documentation writing. In this scenario, user interfaces, program code and configuration file schemas could be ingested by a specialized fine-tuned model, and user documentation or tutorials outputs, such as documents or web sites, could be generated in response. This would have the potential to increase developer productivity by letting the SLM handle repetitive and time-consuming documentation tasks.

For such a specialized model to be created through fine-tuning, sufficient high-quality training data is needed. The agentic training pattern defined in this praxis can address this training problem for documentation generation, and many other domains. This training pattern allows AI engineers to leverage the continually advancing capabilities of commercial LLMs for agentic training. The key advantage is maintaining the bottom-up flexibility of open-source model development of SLMs and ensembles, with their inherent resource efficiency on edge devices – as this praxis has comprehensively addressed.

www.ingramcontent.com/pod-product-compliance
Lightning Source LLC
Chambersburg PA
CBHW071358230926
51846CB00002B/583

* 9 7 8 5 1 6 1 0 6 3 6 7 5 *